FIRESIDE

HEALING STATES

by Alberto Villoldo, Ph.D., and
Stanley Krippner, Ph.D.

Foreword by
Lynn V. Andrews
Author of *Jaguar Woman*

A Fireside Book
Published by Simon & Schuster, Inc.
New York

Library of Congress Cataloging in Publication Data

Villoldo, Alberto.
Healing states.

"A Fireside book."
Bibliography: p.
1. Mental healing.   2. Shamanism.   I. Krippner, Stanley,
date.   II. Title.
RZ400.V5   1987   615.8'52   86-31810
ISBN: 0-671-63202-7

. . . DEDICATED TO THE
HEALING OF THE EARTH.

Contents

FOREWORD

We each need our own unique healing. So often today among people who are familiar with alternative health methods, we hear of the "wounded Healer"—a person who has lived through a life-threatening crisis and has attained special healing power. It is true that each of us, though maybe not a traditional or practicing shaman or healer, is on a journey, seeking wholeness, seeking healing—our own enlightenment. Perhaps this is the true reason that we are on this mother earth, and perhaps enlightenment is the one thing we are most afraid of.

There is a healing sound inherent in each living creature in this universe. The challenge that we each face is to create our own dynamic rhythm in our personal universe. *Healing States* enables us to explore that possibility.

Much has been said about the integrity of modern medicine versus the primal techniques of healing. It is interesting to note that most of the prescribed drugs in use today trace their roots back to medicine plants known for centuries by indigenous cultures and their shamans. If there is one rift between shamanism and modern medicine that I would like to see bridged, it is the one caused by modern medicine's elitism and refusal to communicate. We need the merging of ancient wisdom and modern science. Alberto and Stanley have written a book that provides the accessibility needed for communication between two outwardly disparate yet inwardly common endeavors. That endeavor is the healing of mind, body, and spirit—the healing of the totality of the human organism.

As my teacher, Agnes Whistling Elk, has taught me, we all must make our own act of power in life. This act is essential to provide a mirror for our own behavior and to facilitate our involvement while we also heal others. The art of shamanism is an act of power that long ago initiated the use of healing plants and that teaches us to choreograph the energies held within those plants and within ourselves. We live in a time of vision, a time when all of us are seeking not only new answers but also new questions to help us solve the mysteries that confront us as a species. In *Healing States,* Alberto and Stanley investigate the sources of disease, not just the effects of illness. In doing so, I believe they have addressed one of the most important issues of our time.

Lynn V. Andrews

INTRODUCTION

In 1971, Fred Swinney was told by his physician that he had, at most, three years to live. He was suffering from hypertension, heart disease, ulcers, and hypoglycemia. Seeing a connection between his weakened physical condition and his job pressures as an engineer, he entered psychotherapy. His experience not only improved his physical health but prompted Swinney to enter graduate school in psychology. He received his clinical certification in Transactional Analysis in 1975, and began seeing clients.

But Swinney's career change was only the beginning of a new life direction. In 1976 he was traveling by canoe to James Bay in the wilderness of northern Ontario, Canada. He was alone and had taken along only his sleeping bag and a few supplies. One night Swinney fell asleep before his smoldering fire and had a dream in which animal predators emerged from the woods and devoured him.

Awakening in terror, Swinney cast his gaze toward the coals of the fire. Just beyond he discerned two piercing eyes and the large gray form of a wolf. Swinney's first impulse was to run away but, transfixed by the animal's eyes, found himself unable to move. Surprisingly, a feeling of total surrender replaced Swinney's fear, just as if he were a wolf himself. In the few minutes shared, Swinney experienced a deep union with the wolf. After the wolf disappeared through the trees, Swinney still sensed that he had become a wolf during their brief interaction.

Swinney left the wilderness renewed and grateful to

his inner wolf. He returned to his family and clients in Michigan. But, he asked himself, how could he use the wolf in civilization? As the weeks passed, Swinney attempted to forget the episode as it differed so radically from anything he had ever experienced. He completed his Master's degree in 1980 and avoided any activity or setting that would again evoke his wolflike nature.

Five years later, during a group therapy session held while fire was flickering in Swinney's fireplace, one of his clients expressed extreme anger. Suddenly, Swinney envisioned Libra, the Greek goddess of justice, holding her balanced scales. He asked his client if she could relate to this image. The woman erupted with emotion, telling the group how, during her childhood, her mother had tried to treat her and her sister equally. When the client did not experience this fairness in later life, it upset her and she could not cope with other people very well. Upon working through her memories of her early experiences and subsequent expectations, the client was able to accept the inequities in her relationships. Eventually, she was able to terminate therapy. Swinney realized that the appearance of the image resembled his experience with the wolf. In both instances, he had been brought into direct contact with his feelings, hunches, and intuitions.

Swinney resolved to learn more about wolves. Two friends gave him books about wolves, even though they knew nothing about his experience in the woods or his resolution. His reading provided information about shamans and how they often dream about being devoured and reborn during their initiation rites or training periods. Swinney also learned that shamans were the first professional psychotherapists and that they frequently have "animal guides" that assist their work with clients. Identifying with shamans because of his own "animal guide," Swinney took the name "Graywolf" and introduced shamanic elements into his work as a psychotherapist.

Graywolf shared these experiences with us over the years, and we all planned to meet at the 1984 convention of the Association for Humanistic Psychology in Boston. The program had announced a presentation on shamanism by Stanley Krippner and Alberto Villoldo, but Villoldo's airplane was delayed and Graywolf took his place. Graywolf told his story and led the group in several breathing and imagery exercises that he found useful with his clients. His contributions were well received by the audience of several hundred people, many of whom told Graywolf that they were inspired by his account. This response lent confirmation to Graywolf's direction and he continued to develop his unique approach to psychotherapy. The three of us presented a program on shamanism at another Association for Humanistic Psychology meeting in 1986. By this time, Graywolf's clients considered him a shaman as well as a psychotherapist.

Shamanism is a 100,000-year-old tradition of knowledge that once permeated all forms of medicine and psychotherapy. Shamans were the first healers, responsible for the health and well-being of their community. While today's medical practitioners focus upon clients' physical problems and psychotherapists deal with their mental and emotional difficulties, shamans have always administered to these aspects of their clients' lives as well as to their deep spiritual needs. By "spiritual" we mean those aspects of human experience that reflect a transcendent quality, e.g., an encounter with God, a feeling of unity with all humanity, a connection with life in general and with the universe's creative processes.

The medicine men and women in North and South America believe that all healing involves an experience of the spiritual, where the ill person rediscovers his connection to nature and to the divine. For this, the patient must step out of his ordinary state of awareness and into an extraordinary or ecstatic state where the journey back to health can begin. Don Eduardo Calderon, the Peruvian shaman described in the second part of this book, believes that ill people must also discover their own power as healers, for it is the patients who heal themselves, not the shaman or medical doctor. In this respect, the beliefs of the shamans coincide with those of the spiritual healers, discussed in the first part of this book, who claim that we all have the potential to heal ourselves and others once we discover our source of power and healing in the spirit world and are able to transmit this power to others.

Although the beliefs and healing systems of shamans and spiritual healers are very different, they both believe that we all possess awesome potentials and capabilities, many of which defy our definitions of the normal. They believe that there is life after death, that the mind is able to travel through space to obtain information or influence events happening at a distant location, that one can foretell future events and even change the outcome of these events, that one can travel in dreams, and that one can create one's own healthy body and mind.

The spiritual healers we have studied go so far as to say that unless we develop and train the extraordinary skills and unusual abilities of our minds, these abilities can turn against us, creating psychosomatic disease. Indeed, it appears that the extraordinary capabilities that once were in the exclusive domain of healers, mediums, and shamans have become the birthright of everyone alive today, for we humans are a vital and integral part of the power that animates the cosmos, not something set aside from it.

This shamanic vision has inspired both of us from our earliest years, as one of us [Villoldo] grew up in Cuba in a culture where "spirits" were omnipresent, and the other [Krippner] was raised in Wisconsin where Native American artifacts and traditions were constantly in evidence. We met at the University of Puerto Rico in 1972 when Villoldo was an undergraduate and Krippner a visiting professor. We met again a year later when Krippner was a visiting professor at Sonoma State University in California and Villoldo was studying for his Masters degree in psychology. Eventually, Villoldo completed his doctorate at Saybrook Institute where Krippner was a faculty member.

Over the years, we have marveled at the shamanic legacy that exists in North and South America, as well as at the wisdom in traditions that contain shamanistic elements. We have observed medicine men, medicine women, mediums, and herbalists. We have witnessed their healing sessions, and have attempted to understand their worldview and their models of medicine and psychotherapy. We have seen many of these healers change their state of consciousness through dance, breathing, music, heat, imagery, and herbal preparations, and have sometimes entered these states with them. By "consciousness," we simply mean a person's overall pattern of perceiving, thinking, and feeling. A "state of consciousness" refers to the pattern that exists at any given point in time. Some states of consciousness are said to be especially conducive to self-healing or to the healing of others; these "healing states" require scrutiny whether they involve shamanic rituals, mediumship, or any other procedure.

In the pages that follow we document our journeys and experiences with some of the most extraordinary healers of our time and describe techniques of healing and ecstatic trance that can be used to maintain health and for self-healing. In addition, we have sought to present as accurately as possible the shaman's path to power and knowledge, a path that is undertaken to enable a person to achieve healing and wholeness. We did not always share the healers' interpretation of the events we witnessed, nor do we necessarily agree with everything told us by the healers. Nevertheless, we do harbor a deep sense of respect for the practitioners we have visited and the conviction that their wisdom is again needed on this planet.

Technology and industrialization have produced many benefits for many people. But the earth has paid a price as it suffers from exploitation, erosion, pollution, and overcrowding. A spiritual price has also been paid by those people who feel a lack of connection with anything vibrant or vital in today's world. After more than forty years combined research with spiritual healers and shamans, we are convinced that their healing and spiritual traditions offer a direct and powerful path to the spirit in which, by serving a vision of the vibrant human beings and the harmonious world we can create, we finally learn to take responsibility for the healing and continued evolution of the earth.

Alberto Villoldo and Stanley Krippner

PART I

The Dimensions of Spiritual Healing

In February 1986 newspapers around the world carried photographs of two Amazonian shamans, in full jungle regalia, being received by the president of Brazil. They had left their homes to treat Augusto Ruschi, a renowned naturalist, who was dying from contact with a poisonous toad. Skeptics noted that Ruschi died before the end of the year; advocates of the shamans claimed that the treatment extended Ruschi's life beyond what had been predicted by his physicians. In the same way that Ruschi reached out to alternate health care procedures once allopathic medicine had reached its limits, many other people are beginning to explore the potential benefits of indigenous healers.

The medical establishment in Brazil operates on the same allopathic principles found throughout Western cultures. Disease is usually "caused" by an agent external to the body and must be "fought" with surgery or with drugs that produce effects "different" from the symptoms they treat. (The ancient Greek word *allo* means "other" or "different," hence the term "allopathic.") However, there are a number of "spiritist" groups in Brazil that operate from a different model. They refer many of their clients to homeopathic physicians who use tiny doses of substances in their treatments that produce symptoms similar to the disease (*homeo* means "same" or "similar" in ancient Greek). Their own mode of treatment involves obtaining the cooperation of benign "spirits" and removing the influence of malevolent "spirits."

In the following section we provide a sample of these

3

Brazilian practitioners, including a clinical psychologist claiming to "incorporate" the spirits of famous painters who produce works of art to demonstrate post-mortem survival. We also describe the work of a physician who performs surgery supposedly while guided by spirits who enable him to operate without the use of anesthesia or antiseptics. We share our visits to some of Brazil's most colorful spirit mediums, who permitted us to witness the emergence of their spirit guides. And we portray the innovative procedures of a psychotherapist who trains some of his epileptic patients to become mediums.

No matter what interpretation you want to give these encounters with the spirit world, you will be very impressed by the powers of self-regulation exhibited by these practitioners. Whether someone is painting with both hands in a darkened room, performing a delicate operation with simple surgical equipment, or walking with bare feet over hot embers, the extraordinary powers of the mind/body relationship are at work. Recovering from sickness and maintaining your health can be assisted by self-regulatory powers, and in reading about these healers you might think of ways that you can attain higher states of functioning yourself. Perhaps you can ask your physician how the two of you can work more closely together. Perhaps you can use mental imagery to maintain your well-being. Perhaps you can identify new ways of obtaining sufficient recreation, relaxation, and exercise. "Healing states" are not only applicable to the professional practitioner but also apply to the "inner healer" within us all.

Chapter 1

Life after Life

In the late 1800s the distinguished English scientist Sir Oliver Lodge speculated "If you were to suddenly find yourself in the spirit plane, how would you communicate to your friends and relatives that you were still alive?" Sir Oliver considered a number of possibilities, including leading a friend to a cache of documents whose location was known to no one but him. He realized that this would not constitute proof, as it could be easily explained as a stroke of luck or the result of dowsing, a technique whereby a sensitive person is sometimes able to locate water or lost objects. Neither would transmitting information through a medium—say, the results of one of his experiments—be considered proof, as these were already widely known. Even transmitting to a colleague the idea for a brilliant invention could easily be dismissed as chance or explained as telepathy or even trickery, as were the table rappings that had been so thoroughly discredited at the time.

Sir Oliver's conclusion was that the question of life after death could neither be proved nor disproved. Yet evidence to support the proposition that some element of the personality endures after physical death began to emerge. Frederick Meyers and Edmund Gurney, two early members of the Society for Psychical Research, said that after their deaths they would attempt to communicate through various mediums. For thirty years afterward, several mediums reported receiving messages, typically literary puzzles that made sense only when statements from different mediums were put together.[1] More recently, Ian Stevenson, a psychiatrist, has meticulously gathered data on dozens of cases suggestive of reincarnation.[2]

The Artists and the Psychotherapist

Sir Oliver Lodge's question came to our minds again on a recent visit to Brazil. For example, suppose that you were an artist who suddenly found yourself in the spirit world, and wanted to communicate to your fellow humans that there is life after death: One possibility could be to return to paint new masterworks through a medium or sensitive who would lend his or her hands for communication from the "other world." This is what the purported spirits of Michelangelo, Modigliani, Toulouse-Lautrec, and other renowned artists from the past claim to do as they create new works of art through the medium Luis Antonio Gasparetto, a Brazilian psychologist.

We first met Gasparetto in 1972 when he was nineteen years old and a psychology student at the University of São Paulo. He explained that he had grown up in a family of mediums, and had been incorporating spirits since the age of twelve. Before his twentieth birthday Gasparetto had painted over 2,400 canvasses by over four dozen different artists, each an original signed by the artist— Leonardo da Vinci, Monet, Degas, and others. All the paintings were done in a dimly lit room where one color could not be distinguished from another, and at extraordinary speed, each work being completed in less than ten minutes. Each painting had the unmistakable print of the artist, who sometimes spoke through Gasparetto, offering healing counsel and advice to individuals attending the spirit-painting sessions.

Gasparetto claims he cannot paint at will, that he must set a time when both he and the painters are available, as they lead busy lives in the spirit world. The artists return to help him, he says, "to create a revolution in the way we think about death and about life." He claims that whether one believes in spirits or not, there are many people suffering from illnesses that have their origins in the spirit world. In addition, there are many souls trapped between this world and the next, suffering because they died unconsciously and under the influence of drugs or medication. Gasparetto believes that a little recognized yet essential aspect of healing is for the living to learn how to die peacefully and honorably and the dying to learn to enter consciously into the spirit world.

As a spiritist, Gasparetto believes that the awareness of the continuity of life after death is an essential part of the healing process. Fear in general, but particularly fear of death, is seen as the culprit preventing an ill person from mobilizing all of his or her physical and psychological healing resources. With the awareness of life after death, this burden of fear is lifted, and the person's path to recovery is accelerated. In addition, Gasparetto claims that during the painting session a "window" between the worlds opens and healing energy can flow from the spirit plane to ours, helping to heal physical and spiritual ailments.

Luis Antonio Gasparetto is an accomplished psychologist and today directs a thriving clinic where he treats persons afflicted with psychic and psychological ills. Accompanied by a research group, I (Villoldo) visited his clinic in April 1983 just as his last patient was leaving. We were received by a young psychologist, who ushered us into a large meeting room. She informed us that Luis

Antonio usually worked in the dark, and would be very disturbed by the high-powered lights that we needed to photograph his work. Later, the medium explained that the bright lights burned up the ectoplasm of the visiting spirits, and made it difficult for them to remain connected to his physical body.

The first step in the psychic painting session was summoning the spirits of the painters. Gasparetto closed his eyes and entered into the mediumistic trance, in which he claims to set aside his rational mind so that a foreign intelligence can take over his body. The psychologist had changed from his clinical clothes into paint-stained overalls, and was sitting on a high stool in front of a drawing table on top of which several canvasses had been placed. He asked us to hold hands and form a circle around him, concentrating and sending energy to him. Gasparetto then took several deep breaths, softly praying: "I ask God for the presence of the spirits, the guides, to help us to understand more of the spiritual life, helping to resolve our doubts. In the name of God and the spiritual friends, we can start."

At the end of this invocation, the medium's features appeared to change, his face becoming tense and drawn, and his eyes acquiring a faraway look. One of the assistants turned on classical music, while the medium reached for a blue pastel crayon and began to draw the outline of a figure at a furious pace. The canvas had to be held down or it would have torn from the ferocity of his movements. We stared in silence as he completed a portrait of a young woman and signed it "Claude Monet." The painting was executed in less than five minutes, and Gasparetto had his eyes closed or covered most of the time that he was drawing. He later explained that the paintings had already been completed in the spirit world, and were laid over his canvas like a template. He explained that he simply followed the designs, moving as fast as possible, for his movements were being guided by the "thoughts" of the master who was painting through him.

As soon as he finished the Monet, he began a painting of a young woman with a swanlike, elongated neck. Three and one-half minutes later the portrait was finished and signed "Modigliani, 1983." Like the Monet, the Modigliani signature was identical to the painter's own. So were the color combinations used, and even the models resembled those the artists employed while still alive. "The spirits come to me," Gasparetto explained, "and show their styles, sign their own signatures, and do incredible works. I see Toulouse-Lautrec. I speak with Van Gogh, and these artists want to show that they are still alive, that they preserve their personalities, and that life is eternal. This realization alone can heal the deepest wounds of our spirit."

Gasparetto is not the only psychic painter in Brazil. In 1983, one of us (Krippner) spent an evening with another São Paulo medium, João Pio de Almeida-Prado. Within sixty minutes de Almeida-Prado produced ten credible pastel drawings "signed" by Manet, Picasso, Renoir, Portinari, and others. Later he sold several of his paintings at reasonable prices to members of the group. Gasparetto does not charge money for his trance paintings, as he earns his living from the practice of psychotherapy, but he will accept donations for his charities from people who want copies of his works.

Spiritual Psychotherapy

Gasparetto warns that not all communications from the spirit world are valuable. The mere fact that one has died does not automatically make one wise or holy. As in the ordinary world, in the world of the spirits there are also evil and mischievous beings who can become attached to living persons, and can cause both physical and psychological disease. Persons with highly developed psychic abilities who have "open windows" into the spirit world are most vulnerable to these influences, and often become victims of their own psychic powers. These individuals who are constantly bombarded with unwilling communications from the spirit world make up the majority of Gasparetto's patients.

As a psychologist, Gasparetto must differentiate between psychological illness and psychic or mediumship disorders. He claims that people with severe psychological problems often do not want to be helped. "What we commonly call psychosis," says Gasparetto, "is a personal decision, where one does not want to take responsibility for one's life. When I was at the university I had to go to the mental hospital to study disturbed individuals. Based on my psychic sensitivity, I estimate that 80 percent of the people in psychiatric hospitals today are psychics or mediums who could be healed with the proper education and support."

Gasparetto's clients must also attend one of the six hundred spiritist centers in the city of São Paulo, where they receive psychic healing free of charge. Although they are not required to accept the philosophy of the spiritists, they must accept the possibility that they may possess highly developed psychic abilities. Gasparetto believes that until a person takes full responsibility for his or her unconscious connections with the spirit world, that person will not be healed. He explains that while a trained medium is able to connect with "higher" sources of knowledge and information, an untrained and unconscious medium is at the mercy of these forces, picking up the symptoms from which many spirits still suffer.

During my 1983 visit I (Villoldo) was introduced to Marta, one of Gasparetto's patients who for the past few weeks had been coming to the Spiritist Federation for healing. For several years Marta had been suffering from migraine headaches, insomnia, and general nervous conditions that physicians were unable to identify or treat. After having exhausted all the possibilities of Western medicine, she went to see Gasparetto and was referred to the spiritist center for treatment. The spiritists believe that psychic and mediumship problems affect the entire family, yet manifest only through the most sensitive member of the family. So together with her husband, Marta went to the Spiritist Federation of São Paulo, the largest of all the spiritist healing centers, where over two thousand patients receive treatment daily.

All patients at the Federation must undergo an "entry" interview to determine whether the origin of their disease is physical, psychological, or spiritual. All physical and about 20 percent of the psychological problems are referred to professionals trained in medicine and psychiatry. The reason for this is that the spiritists believe they can effectively treat only those illnesses having a spiritual origin, even though these are often accompanied by physical symptoms including certain cancers, some cases of high blood pressure, epilepsy, and even schizophrenia.

Marta's problem had been diagnosed as "obsession," where a disturbed spirit had become attached to her and was provoking physical and psychological distress. She was unconsciously attracting suffering entities and picking up their symptoms. Marta and her husband were sent to the intensive therapy section, where thirty other persons who also suffered from unconscious connections to "lower spirits" waited. The spiritist explained that "obsession" is a very serious ailment that must be treated early, before it results in irreversible organic disease. One of the healers sat before the group and read passages from the writings of Allan Kardec, the French scholar whose writings have been influential in Brazil. Each person then came to the front of the room for laying on of hands, to balance the subtle energy fields that the spiritists believe surround the physical body, and which form the bridge between the physical and spiritual worlds.

Marta and her husband were then led to a smaller room where three groups of six to seven mediums sat in circles. Marta took her place in the middle of one group of mediums, and her husband in another. Although Marta was experiencing the symptoms, it was possible that the disturbing spirit was a deceased relative or friend of her husband's. The mediums said a silent prayer and began to call on the entity.

Suddenly one of the mediums in Marta's circle bolted upright and with a contorted expression began to speak in a loud and vulgar voice. The female medium had "incorporated" an entity who identified himself as a young man from the north of Brazil who had lost his life in an automobile accident. He last recalled being in a friend's car and seeing a truck swerving onto his path. The young man refused to believe that he had died and claimed that this was only a bad dream from which he would soon awaken. Roberto Rodrigo, the healer in charge of the session, explained that the young man was still in shock and had been attracted to Marta because of her psychic "openness." Through her he could attempt to regain his identity by connecting again with a physical body.

The medium was not able to withstand the force of this spirit inside her, and "passed" the spirit to another female medium in the circle. The young man continued to claim that he was still alive, and laughed at the healer who was explaining to him the events of his death. The healer asked the young man to look down at his body, and in shock he realized that it was the body of a woman, that it was no longer his own. The healers then called on their spirit guides to come to the aid of this confused young man. The spiritists believe that there are hospitals

12

in the other world to help spirits like this be born into the next dimension—they conceive of death as the beginning of a new life. However, whether in this world or in the next, birth is a complicated and often painful affair.

The mediums were careful to point out to us that this was not an exorcism, that their intent was not to toss the spirit of the young man back into the darkness. Their goal was to treat both Marta and the ailing spirit, on whom they conducted "psychotherapy" to help him carry on with his life in the spirit world. They explained that it would take more than one session to free Marta from the offending spirit and bring some relief to the young man.

Was the spirit of a young man truly disturbing Marta, or was this merely a convenient bit of psychological theatrics? In 1976 I (Villoldo) was a speaker at a psychological congress in São Paulo. I took the opportunity to attend a spiritist healing session conducted by a team of medical doctors in order to assist several of their ailing patients. A number of these patients were said to be afflicted by spirits who had died unconsciously and were caught between this world and the next, still experiencing the symptoms of the diseases that caused their deaths.

At the close of the session, after the Lord's Prayer had been recited and the lights were about to be turned on, one of the mediums, an attractive woman in her late thirties incorporated a spirit who began to speak Spanish instead of the Portuguese spoken in Brazil. The spirit began to describe her pain, explaining she was a woman in her seventies who had been hospitalized in an oxygen tent for weeks, and that her lips were dry and her heart ached for her family. The healer in charge of the session explained to her that she had died, that she was now in the spirit plane, and that she was no longer in her former body. To prove it, the healer suggested she examine the

13

medium who had incorporated her spirit. The spirit felt the body of the medium and realized in shock that it was not her own body; these were not her breasts, nor was the dark skin of the Brazilian woman her own.

Suddenly the medium looked in my direction, cried out my childhood name, and ran into my arms, asking where her son (my father) was. She entreated me to help her end her pain; she had been in the hospital too long and wanted to die.

I found myself unable to speak. I simply held the crying woman, unwilling to believe this was my deceased grandmother, yet overcome by the way she called my name as my grandmother (who had died three months earlier) used to. The head of the healing session asked that we send healing energy to this spirit, that she might become conscious of where she was. He explained that by inhabiting the body of the medium, the spirit had regained consciousness and now had to reach a "critical mass" of awareness outside her body so she could complete the journey to the spirit plane. Moments later, the spirit cried out that she could see her own long-dead mother and father (whom she called by name) as well as her husband, all calling to her as if through a translucent veil. The healer instructed her to reach out to them, to allow them to guide her into the next world.

Within minutes the spirit who had identified itself as my grandmother claimed that her pain was diminishing and that she was feeling younger and stronger every moment. The healer told her to imagine herself any age she wished, that her disappearing pain was the result of leaving the physical world; as she reached for her family in the spirit plane she would leave the nightmarish realm between the physical and spiritual worlds behind.

All the while, I had been holding the medium in my arms, tears streaming down my face and unable to say one word. As the group said a final prayer for this spirit, the medium turned to me and still speaking in Spanish said, "Take care of your father, he needs your help. I will always be with you when you need me."

Was this a cleverly devised psychodrama my friends improvised to help me get over my grief at the loss of my grandmother? Although I knew most of the members of the healing group personally, none of them was aware of my grandmother's death or knew her name. Even if they had known of her passing away, they had no way of knowing the name of her deceased husband or relatives. Could the experience be explained as a case of telepathy? In other words, had the healers unconsciously sensed my loss and obtained all the relevant names and information from my own memories?

Regardless of the many alternative explanations for this phenomenon, the experience was not easy for me to dismiss. Moreover, I found it greatly consoling to think my grandmother had been released from her pain.

Messages from Beyond

The artists with whom Gasparetto claims to work bring important messages during the psychic painting sessions. They point out that we live in a society that does not prepare people to die. In our hospitals, we use drugs that confuse the dying, who then enter the spirit world unconscious and unprepared for the next life. These spirits often find themselves trapped between this world and the next in a state of confusion that can last for years. Furthermore, the spirit painters warn us that not all spirits are sources of infinite wisdom. As in the world of the living, there are also dishonest and deceitful spirits, for one does not automatically become "holy" when one dies. In their training, the spiritists must learn to differentiate between the valuable and trivial communications and to make the connections only with the most advanced spirits.

The spirit painters warn that people who have had great mystical fantasies have the most difficult time adapting to the day-to-day realities of the spirit world. On leaving their bodies, they expect to be greeted by Christ sitting on a throne or by the Buddha. Unfortunately, if these individuals led meaningless lives on the Earth, the artists say that this is exactly what they will find in the spirit world. They believe our spiritual work begins on this Earth and continues for all of eternity. Even when they are painting through Gasparetto, such masters as Picasso and Modigliani claim that they are working on their spiritual development by helping us understand that life goes on long after the physical body returns to dust.

Both Gasparetto's parents and grandparents were spiritists and encouraged his mediumship from an early age. He claims that although we have been taught by our religions that we live for eternity, we avoid this issue because, in his words, "We would no longer be able to make decisions without responsibility, not thinking about the future, because life will go on. All the actions we do today will have a reaction tomorrow."

In 1974 Gasparetto was informed by his spirit guides that he should study ballet. This was a baffling communication as he had no predilection for dance. Nonetheless he followed the instructions, and one year later, during a trance painting session, he rolled up his pants cuffs and to everyone's surprise began to paint with his feet. Twelve minutes later he had completed a portrait of a beautiful young woman which he signed "Renoir." He explained that by the time Renoir died, his arms and hands were so atrophied from arthritis that he was forced to paint with brushes tied to his shoulders and elbows.

Since then, we have observed Gasparetto paint as many as three paintings simultaneously: one with his feet, and one each with his left and right hands, each by a different artist. The medium claims that the spirit painters do not need to use his hands, and that his ballet training was to give his feet the movement and dexterity needed to begin painting with them. During a 1983 visit, Gasparetto again demonstrated the ability to paint with his feet. This time he completed a portrait of a young woman, signed "Monet," in less than ten minutes. Gasparetto's hands were always by his side; he picked up the paint, squeezed the acrylic from the tubes, and spread them on the canvas using only his toes.

Other Dimensions of Knowledge

In 1983 our research group observed Gasparetto for over two hours, during which he crafted over a dozen paintings signed by Monet, Picasso, Modigliani, and others. Afterward, the group was curious as to whether the medium had any recollection of what had taken place during the trance painting session. Gasparetto replied that he was awake, yet in an altered state of consciousness. "I feel what they feel," he said, "and I have in my mind their own thoughts. I have no control of my body, but if I want to hold back, I can. Sometimes they come with such beautiful sensations, I see no sense in resisting. And they never come alone, but they come in a group, a very large group of people. I saw dancers in the room, I saw beautiful ladies from the previous century. I am told that they are happy to do this work and I can feel this happiness."

Gasparetto explained that he often felt the impact of four or five personalities at the same time. "They come close to me and hold my shoulders and they control my arms," he said. "But there is also an identification with their feelings and I can sense what they are going to paint. They touch my body and they think that they are doing the paintings and my arms immediately correspond to their thoughts.''

After leaving Gasparetto, one of the scientists in our research group, Dr. George Araki, a biologist from San Francisco State University, commented, ''I suppose that if one were to study and work hard for a very, very long time, one could simulate the work that Gasparetto did, but I don't think that in this case this was a simulation by practicing. He was moving his hands and feet in such a way that I just couldn't believe that he was doing something that he had practiced and rehearsed.''

Not all the reactions from the group were positive. A few people expressed distaste for the idea of mediumship and the thought of having one's mind taken over by another entity. Austrian film producer Georg Lhotsky expressed these feelings most succinctly. He said, ''It could be important to show that there is a pool of consciousness alive all of the time, but I would not like to have uninvited guests in me. I would prefer to be a little-known painter named Lhotsky and not an instrument of Picasso or Monet.''

But as we prepared to leave São Paulo we were struck with the thought that communications from the spirit world could be happening all the time, and that we might simply not be aware of them. Is it possible that many of our intuitions and creative thoughts come from outside ourselves? Although most scientists believe that contacts with spirits are fantasies of the unconscious mind, a small but growing number of investigators believe that the human brain may behave like a complex transmitting and receiving apparatus, which under certain conditions can pick up thoughts from other minds, and even across space and time.

Alternative Theories for Mediumship

The spiritists are not the only practitioners who believe that untrained mental abilities can cause disease. A growing number of allopathic physicians believe that as much as 80 percent of all illness may contain a psychosomatic component. Allopathic medical science, which does not publicly acknowledge the psychic realm, is still at a loss to explain the origin and treatment of many of these psychosomatic disorders, often merely referring to "unconscious conflicts" that can trigger disease. While orthodox medical beliefs tell us to look within for the cause of disease, belief systems like those of the spiritists look "without," into the spirit world, for the cause of certain illnesses. Nonetheless, Western psychotherapy demonstrates that we can find as many "ghosts" and "phantoms" in our inner world of the unconscious as the most enterprising of spiritists finds in the spirit world.

Most psychotherapists use terms like "complexes" and "subpersonalities" to refer to the same causal agents that Gasparetto calls spirits, yet their descriptions are remarkably similar. For example, Carl Jung described "complexes" as partial or fragmentary personalities which have intentionality and are capable of pursuing a goal. They can "upset the stomach . . . disrupt the breathing or disturb the heart."[3] Jung referred to these "figures from the unconscious" as often "uninformed," and resembling descriptions of "the spirit of the departed" which needed to be brought into conscious awareness so that they stop harming the individual.[4] In order to assist his clients to contact their unconscious, Jung often used automatic writing, spontaneous painting, and artistic rituals—all techniques used by Gasparetto and other psychotherapists with a spiritist orientation.

19

The contemporary English healer Matthew Manning was for a time able to paint in the styles of Matisse, Beardsley, Klee, Dürer, and other masters. For him, it was not mediumship but a form of "remote viewing" in which he clairvoyantly scanned paintings and made copies or combinations of them.[5] On the other side of the world, the Soviet psychoneurologist Vladimir Raikov has used hypnosis to facilitate self-confidence and creativity, telling neophyte artists, "You are Raphael," and student pianists, "You are Rachmaninoff." The results are often extraordinary, and Raikov does not attribute the results of his experiments to mediumship.[6] A few art critics have examined these types of paintings, pointing out that art students can produce similar work, often very quickly, and capturing stylistic elements of a master.

But Manning, Almeida-Prado, and Gasparetto had no previous training in art, and would often paint in a darkened room, giving credence to the hypothesis that the human mind may be able to penetrate the barriers of time and space to pick up the thoughts of masters of the past. Luis Antonio Gasparetto may be demonstrating a little-known ability of the mind not only to heal the body, but also to tap into resources of knowledge and creativity that lie beyond our ordinary senses. According to the spiritists, not only do we have this potential within us, but unless we master and train these capabilities of the mind, they may turn against us, causing psychosomatic disease.

In the meantime, some psychotherapists who deal with cases of multiple personality have taken an interest in spiritism. Ralph Allison, an American psychiatrist who has worked with many clients demonstrating this problem, has described the "alter personality" as serving a definite and practical purpose.[7] "Repeatedly," he observes, "I encountered aspects or entities of the personality which were not true alter personalities. . . . I have come to believe in the possibility of spirit possession."[8]

There is always a reason for an "alter personality," usually due to abuse or trauma in childhood. Thus, according to Allison, "The discovery of an entity who doesn't serve any recognizable purpose presents a diagnostic problem. Interestingly enough, such entities often refer to themselves as spirits. Over the years I've encountered too many such cases to dismiss the possibility of spirit possession completely."[9]

Neither Allison nor other investigators report cases of a client's inviting an "alter personality," as Gasparetto and the spiritists do when they purportedly incorporate the more evolved spirits. Although psychotherapists like Allison have been daring enough to consider the hypothesis of spirit possession, there is a need for researchers to investigate the phenomena of incorporation and spirit mediumship, as they may be mechanisms not only for fathoming new depths of the human mind, but also for reaching into new realms of consciousness.*

The Roots of Spiritism

At the Spiritist Federation in São Paulo, close to fifteen thousand people are treated by nearly three thousand mediums every week. Most of the mediums work part-time, and there is no charge for the healing service, hence no pay for the mediums. Donations are encouraged, though, and a wide variety of charitable services

---

* The term "consciousness" is used to refer to a person's overall pattern of perception, thinking, and feeling. Some specific patterns, or "states," of consciousness appear to be especially conducive to self-healing or to the healing of others. These healing states require scrutiny whether they involve mediumship, shamanic phenomena, or any other experience that is of potential value.

are sponsored by the Federation, including homes for the elderly, the handicapped, and destitute children.

The origins of this movement are as curious as the unique foothold it established in Brazil. In the mid-1800s, a French educator had been reading pamphlets on the topic of hypnotism. The educator, whose name was Léon-Dénizarth-Hippolyte Rivail, was convinced that hypnotism was merely a fad, like the even more speculative practices of "table rappings" and "spirit writings" about which he had also been reading. In 1855, he attended a salon in which his hostess introduced the group to the practice of "table rapping." Much to Rivail's amazement, the heavy base of the table appeared to rap against the floor, answering questions and even spelling out messages.

Rivail studied the phenomenon at various homes over the course of a year, and decided that if spirits actually existed, they should be taken seriously. One evening he was given the instruction to hold a pencil and allow the spirits to manipulate his hand to write with it. This worked remarkably well for him, but he noticed that not everyone who tried was able to make a pencil write or a table tap. Rivail reasoned that only certain people were given this ability; he called them "mediums" because they were able to intermediate between humans and the spirit world. As Rivail continued his investigations, a spirit message indicated that he was to take the name of Allan Kardec, supposedly a Druid teacher whose body was occupied by Rivail's spirit during a former incarnation or past life.

Under the name of Allan Kardec, Rivail published *The Book of the Spirits* in 1857; it caused a sensation in France, and later in England, where Kardec's followers were referred to as "spiritists" to distinguish them from "spiritualists"—the term used by an American group of

22

believers who also purported to be able to elicit table raps and otherworldly messages. In 1858, a Brazilian nobleman brought Kardec's book to Brazil and it was an instant success. There were debates about it in magazines and newspapers, and spiritist meetings erupted all over the country. Kardec's later works, *The Book of Mediums* and *The Gospel As Explained by Spirits,* were also successful.

Brazil was an ideal place for Kardec's ideas to take root. The African slaves had brought with them a striking array of deities. Members of the Brazilian upper class, who disliked the enthusiastic dancing and vibrant drum music that accompanied the worship of these African deities, were delighted when Kardec's ideas gained currency. Here was a credo that was suitable to the educated classes. The ceremonies could be held in elegantly decorated homes rather than in barren huts or ramshackle buildings. Furthermore, it had come from France; French was the second language of the intelligentsia and the nobility. The doctrine of reincarnation explained life's inequalities and encouraged followers of Kardec to lead useful lives.

The spiritists taught that the spirit is enveloped in a semimaterial body of its own called the "perispirit" or "etheric body." When a person dies, the "perispirit" can linger on earth, can return to the spirit world, or can reincarnate. Moreover, many diseases are felt to be the result of spirits that remain on earth too long, trying to sap the energy of living people. Spiritist mediums have developed a number of rituals to send these spirits on their way so that they do not afflict the living.

During our first joint visit to the São Paulo Spiritist Federation in 1972, we observed that the ailing person is received by one of the mediums, who makes a quick evaluation of the client. First, however, everyone is sent to an auditorium where a lecture is given about spiritism and the belief that physical illness can reflect spiritual illness. If one does not undergo spiritual growth, the spiritists claim, the physical sickness might return. In each of several rooms, healers use "spiritual passes," a technique where the aura is touched and "massaged" to bring balance to the client's "perispirit."

Another phase of the treatment involves spiritual counseling. The client's problems are discussed and a course of action is determined. Sometimes the advice includes statements "channeled" by spirits through the mediums who sit in another room. Each medium receives a piece of paper with the name of a client. A secretary writes down each statement "channeled" through the medium and this advice is sent to the counselor who is working with the client. Sample readings we have seen have included the following advice:

"Cultivate security. Work toward unity in your family. Produce good vibrations in your home. Reform. Pray. Persevere. See a physician for your ailment. Use homeopathic remedies. Return after seeing a physician."

For especially critical cases, all the mediums might report on the same person and a "majority vote" or even a consensus could be taken on the diagnosis and treatment, and many clients are sent to homeopathic physicians. In a few cases the treatment procedure advises training as a medium. The ability to incorporate spirits is felt to be a necessary part of recovery for some clients, and the illness is considered an opportunity to begin to devote more of oneself to serving humanity.

Thus Kardec's spiritism is more than a spiritual movement. It is a system of social outreach that makes an impact on every aspect of life in Brazil. Yet spiritists believe that we all have the ability to heal ourselves and be a healing influence on others as well as on the schools and other institutions in which we are involved. More-

24

over, the spiritists believe that one can never be fully healed until one becomes a healer oneself, helping the sick and the needy and helping to create a more peaceful and ecologically sound Earth.

Chapter 2

The Medical Doctor Turned Psychic Surgeon

Perhaps the most renowned healer of modern times was Ze Arigo, the son of a Brazilian mechanic, and a man who could barely read or write. Yet in trance, he claimed to incorporate the spirit of Dr. Adolph Fritz, a German physician who supposedly had died in World War I from wounds suffered in a grenade explosion. Both Dr. Fritz and Arigo soon became celebrities, performing surgical operations using only a scalpel or a simple knife that was rarely cleaned and sometimes showed signs of rust. Hundreds of people claimed that the spirit doctor restored their eyesight or removed a cancerous tumor without their feeling any pain during the operations. As Arigo's reputation grew, so did the concern of the Brazilian Medical Association, which eventually pressed charges against him for practicing medicine without a license.

The case made the headlines of every Brazilian newspaper, for although in the 1950s and 1960s Arigo had operated on literally thousands of people, cutting their skin with a rusty surgical scalpel or knife, there had never been complaints concerning infection or death resulting from his operations, and the prosecution could not find a single witness to testify against him. Nonetheless, on the witness stand he admitted to practicing medicine and having prescribed medications and herbal remedies to the people who came to him for healing. However, he claimed that it was not he who was doing the healing, but rather the spirit of Dr. Adolph Fritz. Unable to prove the existence of Dr. Fritz, the reluctant judge sentenced Arigo to a six-month prison term.

The news caused a furor in Brazil, particularly among the poor who made up the majority of his patients. Many protests were lodged against the Brazilian Medical Association. The courtroom marshalls refused to take Arigo to prison, so he walked there himself. At the prison the warden refused to admit him, and when Arigo insisted he be let in, his jailers refused to lock the door to his cell. Soon he began to perform healings on the inmates and guards, and within a few weeks people could be seen forming long lines outside the prison doors in the early hours of the morning, to receive healing by the famous spirit surgeon. Halfway through his sentence, Arigo was released, after a former president of Brazil intervened. A number of articles appeared about Arigo, as well as a popular book,[1] but no research study about his work ever appeared in the medical or parapsychological literature.

Ze Arigo died in an automobile accident in 1971, and was mourned throughout Brazil. In 1980, the spirit of Dr. Adolph Fritz purportedly appeared again, this time operating through the hands of Dr. Edson de Quieroz, a physician working in the city of Recife, Brazil. It appeared as if Dr. Fritz wanted to avoid any further complications with the medical authorities, and therefore chose to work this time with a licensed, practicing physician. I (Villoldo) visited Dr. Quieroz in the spring of 1983 (and Krippner observed Quieroz in 1985),[2] in his clinic where he practices obstetrics and gynecology. When my research group and I arrived we found a half dozen well-dressed women waiting to be examined by Quieroz. One young woman had a child with her, which she informed us had been delivered by Quieroz. She claimed to know nothing about his work as a spiritist surgeon. We were later to learn that his activities as a spiritist surgeon took place at the Spiritist Center downtown, and that in his clinic he practices only conventional medicine.

Once we met, Dr. Quieroz agreed to answer a number of our questions about his work. When I asked if spiritist surgery works in the same way as conventional medical surgery, Quieroz replied, "Only on rare occasions are the techniques the same. In the majority of cases, the methods used by the spirits as they are working through us are very different from the conventional ones known to us in medicine." He went on to explain that he does perform gynecological and obstetrical surgery but "during these surgeries I use all of the conventional medical surgical techniques and with the greatest of caution. I may even be overly cautious because a single misunderstanding by one of my medical patients could have repercussions in my work as a spiritist medium. Some people confuse the activities of the medium and that of the medical doctor and expect extraordinary results from conventional medical surgery.

"I finished medical school in 1975 and completed a year of residence where I specialized in gynecology and general clinical practice. Afterwards, I served for two years in the Army as a doctor. After being in private practice as a medical doctor and surgeon for eight years, I began to work in this experimental and mediumistic work with the spirit of Dr. Adolph Fritz guiding and directing me.

"I see clients in my clinic every day and practice conventional medical surgery two or three times per week. Each day there are mediums at the Spiritist Center who are available for spiritual healing sessions. As a medium, I treat all kinds of illnesses and all pathologies. This is possible because the spiritual team that works with me consists of nearly one thousand medical doctors who once lived on earth and who specialize in different branches of medical science." Quieroz invited us to visit him at the Spiritist Center, where he would be operating the next day.

The Diagnoses

We arrived at the Spiritist Center at the crack of dawn, to be certain we would have sufficient time for setting up our camera equipment. Although Quieroz was not scheduled to arrive for another three hours, and the doors to the Center would not officially open until eight, a long line of people was already forming. Some of them had spent the night under the eaves of the large building, for fear of not having an opportunity for a session. There were old men and women, undernourished infants brought in by their mothers, as well as elegantly dressed middle- and upper-class persons. We learned later that several were medical doctors. Some had come out of curiosity, and some to receive surgery, believing there was less risk in a spiritual operation than in the conventional medical surgery they knew firsthand. By the time the Center doors opened there were more than two hundred people in line. The patients were each given a number and told to wait for their turn.

When Quieroz arrived we were led to a large room where a circle of mediums sat absorbed in prayer and meditation. After Quieroz took his seat in the circle, the director of the Center began the Lord's Prayer and asked the mediums to call on their own spiritual teachers. They were also asked to call on the spirit of Dr. Fritz to take over the body of Edson de Quieroz. Within minutes, Quieroz's body convulsed, his facial expression changed as his mouth became drawn and his eyes opened wide. When he spoke, his voice was no longer the voice of Quieroz, but a gruff voice with a heavy German accent. He walked over to us and asked who we were. He introduced himself as Dr. Adolph Fritz.

During the next three hours the Center was buzzing with activity. In a makeshift examining room, Dr. Fritz received each client, often diagnosing them in less than three minutes, and prescribed medication for their condition. His assistants, two nurses and a physician, wrote out directions for the use of the pharmaceutical and herbal remedies that were prescribed. Often the prescription was for a drug popular in the early 1900s but not available today. In these cases, Quieroz's assistants would find a more contemporary substitute.

We asked the assisting physician how Dr. Fritz could diagnose so rapidly. He explained that the diagnosis had already been done in the spirit plane, and that Dr. Fritz was simply communicating the results of examinations performed by his colleagues in the spirit world. Every once in a while Dr. Fritz would indicate that a client should step into an adjoining room, explaining that his or her condition required surgical intervention.

The Operations

By 11:00 A.M. the diagnoses and prescriptions had been made, all without charge, as both Quieroz and the members of the Spiritist Center contribute their time free to this work. In the next five hours Dr. Fritz would operate on about twenty patients without using specialized instruments, anesthesia, or the slightest concession to cleanliness or hygiene. We were told that of the thousands of persons Dr. Fritz has operated on through Quieroz's hands, there has never been a case of infection or death.

It was past noon, the sun was at its hottest, and the operating room, a small cubicle twenty feet by ten, was crammed full of people, including some guests of Quieroz and the members of our research team. In addition, the 6,000 watts of cinematic lights we needed to film the operations made the heat in the little room almost unbearable, and everyone, including Quieroz, was bathed in sweat.

The first client was Agenor Silva, an attorney in the city of Recife who had suffered three heart attacks in recent years. Although he was not a spiritist, he explained that he chose to be operated on by the spirit of Dr. Fritz because of the risk involved in conventional surgery. He was asked to lie down on a narrow cot in the center of the room that served as the operating table.

The surgeon told Silva to take off his shirt, breathe deeply, and relax. The nurse began to shave Silva's chest. Like most of the clients whom we observed, Silva was calm and confident despite the knowledge that he would be operated on with a dirty scalpel that had already been used on half a dozen other patients.

"The shaving of his chest is turning out to be bloodier than the surgery," remarked the surgeon, noticing that the nurse had accidentally nicked Silva while shaving his chest. "The surgery I am going to perform involves an operation on a 'body' that many people are ignorant about and that modern medicine does not recognize. My surgery involves the spiritual body or perispirit, as well as the physical body. The spiritual or etheric body is much more sensitive than the physical one. The etheric body never dies, but continues to develop throughout eternity."

As he reached for the dirty scalpel, the surgeon turned

to Silva and said: "Think of God the Father. Don't worry about anything." Holding the scalpel over the heart, he proceeded to make a six-inch-long incision in Silva's chest, cutting repeatedly with the sharp instrument to a depth of about one-quarter inch. Silva remained unperturbed, with his eyes closed as if he were in a deep trance.

The surgeon inserted three syringe needles, each over one and one-half inches long, into Silva's chest. He claimed the blockage in the artery had been compressed to a fraction of its normal size and could easily ooze out of a needle. A dark mass began to emerge from one of the needles. It was a thick material which did not resemble blood. "What is happening now," explained Dr. Fritz, "is a process of dematerialization of the material that was obstructing the artery."

Even with an incision in his chest a quarter of an inch deep, Silva was tranquil and did not flinch when the spiritist surgeon passed the hand of a visiting physician over the cut to demonstrate it was real. Less than a minute later, the surgeon removed the needles and claimed that the operation was finished but that the healing process would continue over the next few days. Less than one hour after the surgery we asked Silva whether he had felt any pain and he responded, "No, I felt fine, very tranquil. I was prepared spiritually for this operation."

Earlier that day we had seen the surgeon operate on a woman with a severe cataract in one eye. Dr. Fritz explained that this was a thin layer of cells that had grown over the lens, making the eye opaque and greatly reducing the woman's vision. To our horror, he then reached for a surgical clamp and deftly pincered the tissue that had grown over the lens of the eye! In less than three minutes he had cut off the superfluous tissue, without scratching the cornea, and bandaged the woman's eye.

We learned that the woman's vision improved significantly over the following weeks.

Dr. Fritz then explained that the limits of spiritual surgery were directly related to the degree of faith of the client. We asked whether the healing still worked even if the person had no faith. "That is relative," he answered, "because the faith that the religious man likes to talk about is one kind of faith and is different from faith in the practical sense. At the moment of the spiritual operation, you can be a crass materialist and still have the faith required for someone to achieve success in the healing. Faith doesn't mean religious knowledge, nor do you find it within a church or a temple. True faith is something else. Faith is that inner commitment to life that brings emotional balance to the person."

The next client was a woman suffering from infectious sinusitis. She reclined on the bloodstained cot, appearing confident. The surgeon sprayed a decongestant into her nose, his fingers bloodstained from the previous operation, and asked the nurse for clamps. "These are normal surgical clamps without teeth," he said, and explained that she had a deviated septum, which was the cause of the chronic sinusitis with recurrent infections. He clamped a piece of cotton with the instrument and inserted it four and a half inches into her nose, so that all we could see was the base of the instrument, which the surgeon proceeded to twist inside her nasal passages.

"Swallow, swallow," requested Dr. Fritz. "Can you feel blood?" The woman nodded her head, remaining completely calm, the only sign of discomfort being a single tear that ran down the side of her face. There were several medical doctors witnessing the operation, who commented how difficult it is to insert such large surgical clamps into the nasal passage without causing serious damage.

When the surgeon extracted the clamp, the piece of cotton was drenched with blood. "You can get up now," he said, and instructed the patient to relax and keep her head back. As she sat up on the operating table we asked her how she felt. "Good, very good," she replied. "I felt no pain, it was like being under anesthesia. I was so tuned into God that I did not feel anything."

The next client was a woman who had been diagnosed as suffering from breast cancer, and who had chosen to come to the spiritist doctor rather than lose her breast in conventional surgery. She was a large woman in her late forties, a housewife who lived on the outskirts of the city. Her regular physician had already scheduled her for a radical mastectomy at the local hospital. As she took off her blouse and covered herself with a towel, she explained that although she was a spiritist, she was only a neophyte.

The surgeon felt the tumor with his fingers and massaged the woman's breast (he claimed to be able to induce a spiritual anesthesia merely by touching the body). Dr. Fritz explained that the tumor was rigid and adherent, and that it would be a difficult operation. He told the woman to think about the Lord.

Holding the scalpel in his right hand, the surgeon made a deep incision on the woman's right breast. From our vantage point less than two feet away from the patient, we were able to see him cut through the skin until he reached the inner tissue of the breast. The client had been moaning, complaining that it hurt and that she could not tolerate the pain. Yet to our surprise, her body remained calm and relaxed, and she offered no resistance. This was one of the few instances in which we saw one of Dr. Fritz's patients in pain, although the pain was not intense enough for her to be restrained. Dr. Fritz explained that he was rupturing major blood vessels, yet

34

there was little bleeding even in such a sensitive area as the breast.

Next the surgeon inserted his finger inside the cut, and began to pry the tumor out, using only his index finger and thumb, which were still stained with the blood of the previous operations. A few minutes later he removed a tumor the size of a golf ball, and handed it to a pathologist for laboratory analysis. The laboratory results would show that the tumor was cancerous.

The entire surgery took less than six minutes. After extracting the tumor, Dr. Fritz turned to one of the visitors observing the operation, Dr. Pablo Ortiz, a Brazilian surgeon, and asked him to place his fingers inside the incision. Dr. Ortiz reported: "I am a surgeon and I can tell you that one can perceive more clearly with the hands than with the eyes in situations like these. With my fingers I felt the cavity where the tumor had been and I saw the tumor come out. What I perceived was a medium-sized tumor, part of which had been lodged in the upper right quadrant. It would have been difficult to remove. Probably in ordinary surgery it would have required complete removal of the breast. I also noticed something very interesting. As I could see it, when you operate with your fingers instead of with instruments, you do less damage to the tissue."

The spiritist surgeon appeared to be in no hurry to bandage the woman, taking the time to explain that in conventional Western surgery, the woman would have lost her breast. When he completed his short lecture he proceeded to clean the area with a towel, wiping the blood that remained on the woman's chest. He then simply bandaged the cut, using no suture or stitches of any kind, and commented that the cut would heal by itself in the following week. Half an hour later we interviewed the patient as she was sitting in the recovery room. When we asked if she felt any pain, she responded, "No, just a slight tickling sensation. I feel totally normal. I have to give thanks first to God and then to Dr. Fritz.'' We followed the patient's progress over the next two years, and, as of our last contact, she appeared to be fully in remission, with no recurrence of the cancer, and enjoying excellent health.

One of the members of our team, Dr. George Araki, monitored the woman's pulse, and was surprised to find that during the operation her pulse was so faint that it was difficult to detect. Dr. Araki would later comment: "We have, in the United States, focused on far too narrow means of healing, the physical, the chemical— drugs, and surgery. I think these are too limited a frame of reference for a holistic healing system.''

Dr. Fritz claims that he was a surgeon killed during World War I. Curiously, the surgical techniques of Dr. Fritz resemble those used by surgeons in the battlefield, where they must operate with great speed, without complex instruments, and often with no anesthesia or hygiene. Even in the most complex of Dr. Fritz's surgeries, we observed little bleeding, and at no time did he use stitches to close a cut.

Next, an elegant and attractive woman in her late thirties made her way through the crowd of people to the operating table and greeted Dr. Fritz. She turned out to be a medical doctor on whom the surgeon had operated eight days earlier, removing a large lipoma below her left shoulder blade. The woman agreed to allow us to examine her scar, which appeared to be three to five days old, with regular edges and no sign of infection or swelling. What impressed us the most was that even though the cut was at least three inches long and relatively deep, the spiritist surgeon had used no suture to close the skin. We asked the patient, Dr. Louise (she requested us to withhold her last name for fear of recrimination from the

Brazilian Medical Association), why she had chosen to have her tumor removed by Dr. Fritz and not by conventional surgery, as this was a relatively routine operation for Western medicine. "Because I have great respect for the dangers of anesthesia," she replied.

We then asked her why the scar from the spiritual operation had not yet healed. Dr. Louise replied, "Because scarring occurs in several ways. In this case it is not a normal healing but one that follows the mediumistic system, a system that is beyond my ability to explain." Seeing that we were somewhat baffled by the term "mediumistic system," Dr. Fritz explained that there are instruments and sterile gauze and drugs being used, but they are in the spirit plane, and cannot be perceived in the material world.

We asked Dr. Fritz if he ever had any casualties or failures in his spiritual operations. "There are no failures in spiritual surgery, no matter what techniques are used," he replied. It can happen, though, in the case of a patient who does not follow the indications for the rest and diet after the operation, or who may put a dirty finger into an eye that has recently been operated on while scar tissue is still forming. The lack of respect for these directions can cause an organic reaction that can be a risk to the treatment. Yet this is not malpractice by the team of spirit surgeons.

Quieroz has organized a research department and has begun collecting some data. Until the data have been analyzed, it is not possible to determine the exact success rate of his operations. In the meantime, we can only speculate. His ability to diagnose and perform surgery rapidly may be an example of *state-dependent learning,* a condition in which people can learn a task while drugged or hypnotized that they cannot perform in ordinary consciousness. However, they can recall the task and perform it again when they reenter the altered state. Of course, Quieroz's medical training has provided him with the basic surgical skills he needs for the spiritist surgery.

State-dependent learning also characterizes many cases of multiple-personality disorders, a condition in which an individual manifests two or more distinct personalities. State-dependent learning might also explain Gasparetto's painting ability which is virtually absent in his ordinary conscious state. Each subpersonality, when dominant, determines that person's attitudes, showing relatively distinct behavioral patterns. In some subpersonalities, amnesia exists for the thoughts and actions of the other subpersonalities. Some "alter personalities" may try to sabotage, dominate, or destroy the "host personality."[3]

In the case of mediumistic incorporation, the spirit appears to facilitate the functioning of the medium. Rather than being conceived as an instance of multiple-personality disorder, the relationship between Quieroz and Dr. Fritz (and Quieroz's other spirit guides) can better be described as a case of what psychologists often call *co-consciousness,* in which more than one consciously experiencing psychological entity can exist within a healthy human organism. Each personality has some sense of its own identity or selfhood despite their relatively separate and discrete identifications.

This is another example where cross-cultural research could teach us a great deal about the human psyche. But instead of seeing the advantages of Quieroz's work, the Brazilian authorities have reacted negatively. The state where he lives has even moved to rescind his medical degree, on the grounds that Quieroz employs "unorthodox methods." Yet hundreds of people continue to seek his help, including a growing number of medical doctors who are increasingly wary of the dangers of orthodox surgery.

Chapter 3

The Spiritual Psychiatry of Dr. Mendes

For the last two hundred years Western medicine has rejected the idea that illness is caused by spirits. Nonetheless, so-called "incurable" diseases are being successfully treated by a medical doctor who believes in the power of the spirit world. Dr. Eliezer Mendes, a surgeon by training, has exchanged the scalpel for a more spiritual type of intervention. For the last fifteen years epileptics have been coming to Dr. Mendes's clinic outside São Paulo, often leaving a few months later as highly trained psychics, free of medication and with no further symptoms.*

---

* Western medicine considers epilepsy to be a disorder of the central nervous system associated with abnormal electrical activity of the brain. Symptoms include seizures, episodes of confusion, periods of unconsciousness, and unusual sensations—everything getting larger or smaller, lighter or darker, louder or more quiet. Physicians take the position that anything that damages nerve cells in the brain can cause epilepsy; in addition, some cases are felt to be hereditary and about 10 percent are of unknown origin. Epilepsy can usually be controlled by antiepileptic drugs, many of which have unpleasant side effects. Surgery is helpful in some cases, but the aging process has the best curative effect, 75 percent of the cases clearing up within ten years after the onset.[1]

39

Although trained in allopathic medicine, Dr. Mendes has practiced nontraditional healing almost exclusively for the last fifteen years. During this period he claims to have had more than an 85 percent success rate in the healing of epilepsy. I (Villoldo) have known the doctor for over ten years, and Krippner interviewed him in 1985. Although we cannot verify Dr. Mendes's claims fully, we have seen and heard testimony from countless patients who report complete cures. In recent years he has also begun treating schizophrenics and persons with multiple-personality disorders, using the same medium-ship healing techniques, albeit with lower success rates. He believes that these and other illnesses can be caused by intrusive spirits that are attracted to patients who have "open windows" into the spirit world. Through mediumship training they learn to control the "opening" and "closing" of these psychic channels, and to select only the highest forms of spirit communication.

In 1983, after driving for nearly two hours from downtown São Paulo, our (Villoldo's) group reached a small valley where the clinic is located. We were impressed by the beauty of the surrounding mountains, and with how the institution resembled a health spa more than a clinic. Mendes explained that being in a natural environment was an essential element of his healing method. The clinic was designed as a therapeutic community where both therapists and persons who have been diagnosed as schizophrenics, multiple personality cases, and epileptics can live together, and where the patients have a great degree of freedom. Indeed, when we arrived, there were over a dozen persons walking or sitting on the lawns or by the swimming pool. Nearly half of these were therapists, who ate, lived, and worked together with the patients. Furthermore, Mendes emphasized that the word "patient" was not used in the clinic, as this implied that

40

the person depended on a "doctor" for his or her healing. Instead, the "guests" attending the clinic were encouraged to come with their families, often staying for less than one month. They were continually reminded that they were responsible for their own healing and that no one was going to magically cure them. Instead, they had to develop their psychic abilities and learn to manipulate the spirit world, and not have the spirit world manipulate them.

Shortly after our arrival, we gathered with Mendes and a dozen of his "guests" on the clinic grounds. Mendes explained, "We encourage our guests to give full expressions to their problems. You could say that we encourage the full expression of madness and of epilepsy. We then give them bioenergetic and psychic exercises that correct their improper use of altered awareness. After many years of observation, we have come to the conclusion that epilepsy, schizophrenia, and multiple-personality disorders can all result from inappropriate states of consciousness. Therapeutic exercises help to organize the guest/patients' psychic energies and teach them to manage their highly developed yet poorly trained mediumship and trance abilities."

Mendes learned his healing methods from the Umbanda religious tradition (see Chapter 4), where an adept enters into an ecstatic trance in which he or she claims to have direct contact with the spirit world. Early in his medical career, while still a surgeon, Mendes participated in and eventually became head of an Umbanda group. He observed that when a person first became a medium, he or she often would have epileptic-like seizures. At other times, certain aspects of the medium's personality would become exaggerated; he or she would begin to hear voices and see visions, and would demonstrate some of the symptoms of schizophrenia or multiple personality disorder.

In both cases these symptoms would result from the first shocking contact with a disembodied spirit, when a foreign intelligence entered the novice medium's body and created epileptic-like seizures, loss of contact with external reality, or a "double" personality. All of these symptoms were said to stop as soon as the medium developed his or her psychic abilities and learned to regulate his or her "open window" into the spirit world. Mendes claims that these symptoms could also be caused by traumas from one's own past lifetimes, particularly when one suffered a shocking or painful death. These personalities from one's past could act as foreign entities that intrude on one's psyche, and must be dealt with as intrusive spirits. While Mendes has eliminated many of the ritual aspects of Umbanda, he still relies heavily on its healing and mediumship techniques to deal with these intrusive personalities.

One of the first patients we met at the clinic was Oscar Sanchez, a fifteen-year-old epileptic. One month earlier, he and his mother, father, and brother had spent two weeks in the clinic learning mediumship techniques to help control the boy's convulsions. Mendes believed that Oscar's epilepsy was caused by a disturbing spirit that affected the entire family but expressed most through Oscar. Mendes explained that the disturbing spirit and Oscar were vying for the same nervous system, triggering the electrical storms in the brain that manifested as epilepsy.

The family had returned for a weekend of follow-up with Dr. Mendes. Mrs. Sanchez explained to us that Oscar's seizures appeared rather suddenly at an early age. They had become increasingly acute and unmanageable in the last few years, despite the anticonvulsive medication he was taking. Oscar said that before coming to the clinic, he had been having seizures almost every week.

"It was very difficult to carry out ordinary activities," he said. "When I came here and stopped taking medication, I had some terrible epileptic crises, but after ten days of treatment, they subsided and I have had no problems since." Oscar's mother explained that from the age of five her son had had to take very strong medication to control his seizures. But the medicine interfered with his schoolwork to the point where he could no longer lead an ordinary life. When they came to Mendes's clinic one month ago, she stopped his medication. According to Mrs. Sanchez, "His improvement was total. He has no more seizures, he practices sports, goes to school again, and leads a normal life at home."

But Mendes pointed out that he did not consider the success of the last few weeks as evidence of a complete cure. In many cases, he said, "the symptoms disappear quite quickly. We must have a longer period of observation before we can say that he has been successfully healed. After we removed all medication, Oscar entered into a crisis where we encouraged him to let the seizures appear and learn to control them."

When we asked if learning to control the seizures constituted the basis of the treatment, Mendes explained that control is not the issue—as the basis of his therapy is hypnotic regression. This regression can take the patient back to childhood, or to a prenatal state when the person was still inside the womb, or even to former lifetimes.

Mendes believes that, to cure themselves, most epileptics must discover and resolve the highly charged emotional events that contribute to their illnesses. But, unlike conventional psychotherapists, he feels that these traumatic events may have happened in another lifetime. He explained that Oscar's seizures were caused by an intrusive personality—a former lifetime in which he was a young woman who was raped and later beaten to death.

43

As soon as Oscar reached puberty, this former personality emerged from his unconscious and sought to manifest itself.

Mendes explained that to eliminate Oscar's seizures, this former personality had to be healed from the traumatic experience that had caused its death. The healing would be accomplished by having one of the clinic's mediums incorporate the former personality and help her psychologically integrate and discharge that experience, just as if it had happened in this lifetime. Like the Kardec spiritists, Mendes believes that there is life after death and that the spirit goes on to live in another dimension after the loss of the physical body. He also believes that certain physical and psychological problems can become part of one's subtle energy field and can manifest again when one reincarnates, as in Oscar's case.

With the help of African and Brazilian drum music, Dr. Mendes hypnotizes his patients so that they can experience a regression to their childhood, and even to former lifetimes. Being a physician, Mendes does not rely on ritual paraphernalia such as candles, rattles, and spears, as the Umbanda mediums do, but on hypnotic regression. When the client has regressed to the traumatic event that is causing his or her ailment (such as freezing to death in the woods, or being killed in battle), a medium is called in to incorporate the patient's past personality or a disturbing entity and to discharge and release the entity through a psychotherapeutic process.

Mendes believes that the releasing of a disturbing spirit or of a painful event from the past (where one's own former personality becomes the "disturbing spirit") offers only temporary relief. Unless the client learns to master his or her own psychic abilities the condition will reappear. Therefore Mendes insists that mediumship training be part of the therapy, for often a person's highly developed yet poorly trained psychic faculties will produce a variety of psychological and physical diseases.

Mediumship Training

Some past lives have such a powerful influence, Mendes claims, that if they are accidentally awakened they can behave like separate personalities and can take over one's will. "You can be possessed by a past life of your own," he said, "living over and over again a painful death, like Margot is doing." He pointed to a thin young woman sitting near us on the lawn in front of the main house that served as the activity center for the clinic. He explained that Margot had been employed in a government office until she suffered a schizophrenic episode and was sent to a psychiatric institution. A month earlier, her sister Suzanne had brought her to Mendes's clinic for treatment. Because Mendes believes that families often reincarnate together to work out problems from the past, he asked Suzanne to remain at the clinic to facilitate her sister's treatment.

A small group of patients gathered around us on the lawn. Margot came over, sat on Mendes's lap, and began to giggle shyly. Although she seemed to be a happy person, Mendes explained that Margot was sometimes full of hatred toward others. "She is living in her own reality," he commented. "She is like a child, that's why she likes to sit on my lap. She frequently creates scenarios between a father and a daughter, as she is doing with me now. She is regressing into her infancy in a former lifetime. Many people categorized as schizophrenics exhibit the same pattern of being trapped in a former life," he explained.

We asked Mendes what kind of treatment he would follow with Margot. "This young woman is Margot's sister," he replied, pointing to an attractive blond woman. "While participating in the therapeutic exercises with Margot, Suzanne also developed her abilities as a medium. The idea is now to transfer the 'madness' from Margot to her sister through the process of mediumship." In other words, with her new mediumship abilities, Suzanne would incorporate the spirit that was supposedly causing her sister's schizophrenia. It was alleged that in this case the "spirit" was one of Margot's past lives in which she had suffered a traumatic death by drowning. This incident had been awakened from her unconscious a few years previously and had haunted her relentlessly since.

We asked Suzanne if she did not think it was dangerous for her to take on her sister's madness. "I am not afraid," she answered. "I began to develop my abilities only one month ago. I learned to pick up energies from my sister and from other patients, and then to release them."

Mendes explained how Suzanne was trying to eliminate the "intruding" spirit that had rooted itself in Margot's psyche. "An intruding personality," he noted, "is an energy that has an identity of its own and usually presents itself as a person—a living or a dead person. This energy can influence another person's mind and emotions. To achieve the healing of our patients, we must liberate these intrusive energies either by the patient's own efforts or with the aid of a medium that can capture these energies and transform them." Mendes went on to say that although no one knows exactly how the phenomena of mediumship work, the important point is that it has proven useful in treating these disorders. "Every time Suzanne incorporates her sister's madness," Mendes said, "she helps to discharge the energy complex that has left Margot psychologically paralyzed.

We hope that over the next few weeks Margot will become psychologically functional again.''

The epileptic and schizophrenic patients and their family members who had been attentively listening nodded in agreement. Obviously they all shared the belief that their own disorders could also be caused by disincarnate spirits or traumatic events from their former lifetimes. At this point a young man who had been diagnosed as schizophrenic spoke up, and to everyone's amazement said, ''I believe Mendes is the craziest of us all. To treat what people normally call madness and to treat it without drugs, without doping people up, but by cultivating madness and playing with madness, he has to be much, much crazier than we are.''

Regression to Past Lives

Later that afternoon, one of the therapists led us to a large room in the main building of the clinic, and explained that a therapy session would begin shortly, where over thirty patients and family members would regress to their pasts to search for and discharge the repressed traumas that caused a patient's epilepsy or schizophrenia. As the patients and family members arrived, they settled against the walls and engaged in small talk. They all appeared comfortable, though slightly anxious. One of the therapists explained that the patients are free to come and go as they wished, as Mendes considers the desire to be healed an important criterion when working with epileptics, schizophrenics, and multiple personality cases. Another important consideration is that family members are required to take part in the therapy sessions as well as in the mediumship training, for Mendes believes that healing can only take place within the context of the family.

The last person to walk in was Margot, the young schizophrenic woman we met earlier. (Mendes reminded us that although the patients had been medically diagnosed as schizophrenic, epileptic, or suffering from multiple-personality disorders, they are not labeled as such in his clinic. He feels that these labels are derogatory and hinder instead of help the healing process.) Mendes explained that Margot was approaching a turning point in her therapy—she was beginning to comprehend how she had been trapped by an aspect of her past.

The group joined hands, formed a circle around the room, and began to move to the rhythm of samba music that played through the loudspeakers. One by one, Mendes spun patients and relatives around the center of the room. They continued to spin counterclockwise in circles in the same manner that Umbanda mediums do when they enter into trance. While spinning in circles is a technique commonly used by Sufi dancers and in various shamanic traditions throughout the world for entering altered states of consciousness, Mendes has added a unique variation. At times the people in the group would break out into spontaneous dance. Mendes explained that this helped to relax the body and release any physical tensions. After an hour the music became softer, and the dancers reclined exhausted on the floor.

Next to each patient was a family member and a medium. The medium's job was to incorporate, reexperience, and then discharge the past lives and disturbing spirits that were felt to cause the patient's illness. The group began to breathe rhythmically (which helped each person enter into trance) as Mendes went to each individual and stimulated his or her "third eye." He called upon them to open up their inner vision and journey into the past, where they might discover the origin of their disease. One by one the mediums began to moan loudly, some breaking into tears. Mendes approached each medium and spoke to the entity the medium had incorporated, performing psychotherapy with the purported spirit or former incarnation.

At one point, we noticed that Margot was sitting and screaming at her sister Suzanne, telling her to go away and never come back again, and to leave her alone. Mendes explained that Suzanne, acting as a medium, had taken on the cause of her sister's "madness," the past incarnation in which Margot had suffered a traumatic death by drowning. It was as if Margot were looking at her past life in a three-dimensional mirror, trying to break away from it, and screaming at it to leave.

Meanwhile, Suzanne was lying on the floor, her body convulsing in spasms, pounding her fist on the carpet and screaming that she did not want to go back and drown again, that she wanted to live, and not swallow any more water. Mendes explained that Margot had been constantly reliving this experience of death by drowning that Suzanne was now trying to discharge. Suzanne struggled to hold on to someone or something, and grabbed the hand of a young man, asking him for help. At that moment Mendes began rubbing her forehead to help her disconnect from her sister's traumatic death. Slowly, Suzanne returned from the trance, exhausted from the experience. Mendes commented that Margot would again be "possessed" by her own past, hating the personality that had again taken her over and resenting her sister for not removing the pain permanently. This cycle could only be broken if Margot herself were eventually able to disengage from her former lifetime, but for the moment, she lacked the psychological strength to do this, so her sister had to symbolically do it for her.

As the music stopped, Mendes helped each medium and patient come out of the trance that they had been in for over one hour. Gradually people opened their eyes and began speaking with each other, comparing experiences and sharing what they thought and felt. Later that evening the group met with Mendes to discuss and analyze their inner journeys.

Not until weeks later, when we carefully studied our films and audiotapes, did we fully understand what had happened in the therapy, for chaos had reigned in the room for over an hour. About fifteen mediums purportedly had incorporated disturbed entities or past lives of the patients. The mediums were crying, moaning, and talking simultaneously. Yet Mendes appeared to be in control of the situation at all times, sometimes working with the medium, sometimes with the patient who lay entranced on the floor, and always taking time to explain to us what was going on. It was easy to see why a visiting skeptic could misinterpret what happened in these sessions, dismissing it as a cult practice or a disguised Umbanda session.

After the session itself, we had asked Suzanne and Margot to join us outside on the lawn. We wanted to know what had taken place during the regression, and if Suzanne remembered what happened while she was in trance. "I do not remember everything," she said. "I felt an energy, but I did not know who it was. I felt that someone was pulling my hand. I felt a force pulling me. But I feel I am developing psychically every time I work." She recalled more bodily sensations than anything else, yet was unable to fully describe what she felt. What was most important, she said, was that she was helping her sister, "but now I am finding that I am also liberating myself. It is not only that I am picking up and releasing intrusive energies, but I am also liberating my own. I am increasing my freedom."

Mendes believes that mediumship can have both medical and psychotherapeutic value. "The importance of mediumship," the physician explained to us as we sat on the lawn outside the clinic, "is that it teaches people to

Painting done by psychologist/spirit painter Luis Gasparetto using only his feet. It is signed "Monet."

Painting signed "Toulouse Lautrec" completed by Gasparetto in under four minutes.

Painting signed "Modigliani" completed by Gasparetto in under four minutes.

Gasparetto takes bold strokes without looking as he completes a drawing signed "Picasso."

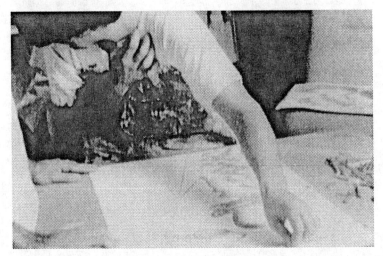

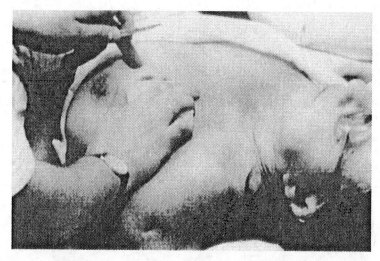

Edson Quieroz, M.D., guided by the spirit of Dr. Adolph Fritz, makes an incision on the patient's breast.

Dr. Quieroz (extreme left), *in trance, removes a tumorous cancer from the patient's breast.*

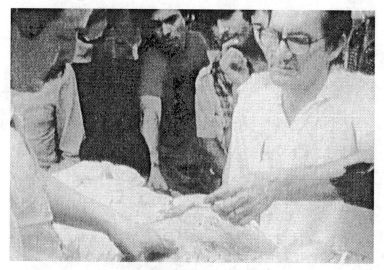

Medium/therapist in Dr. Eliazer Mendes's clinic helps an epileptic enter into trance.

In Dr. Mendes's clinic, three female mediums make a "star" formation, holding their heads next to a male patient to incorporate a disturbing spirit entity.

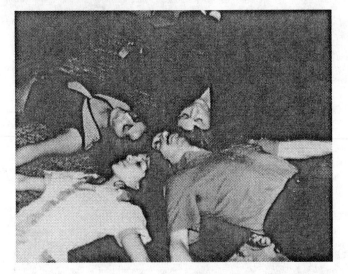

Dr. Mendes and Marta, a young schizophrenic patient.

Healing room in Umbanda Center.

Umbanda five-pointed star used to channel cosmic healing energies.

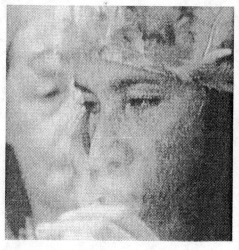

Don Roberto, incorporating the spirit of Peña Azul, extends a blessing to the congregation.

An Umbanda medium has incorporated the spirit of an Indian healer and smokes a ceremonial cigar.

Umbanda mediums twirl as they enter into trance.

Yemanja, Goddess of the Waters and Patroness of the Candomble temple.

Final moments of the initiation ritual at the Temple of Yemanja.

Opening prayers for the firewalking ritual.

The burning coals are spread to cover an area measuring 10 feet by 21 feet.

Wearing the robes of a peasant, Bhuddist monk Siba dashes across the burning coals.

Participants walk across burning coals as a monk feeds rice to the spirit of the Dragon that lies over the coals.

work with their own energies. Mediumship is a biophysical practice that takes people into transcendental states where they begin to explore their extraordinary abilities and other dimensions of their emotions and thoughts. Mediumship results in an integration of the physical, mental, emotional, and spiritual sides of the person. It is, therefore, a transcendental integration of the personality.''

During this time Margot had been looking at Suzanne with obvious scorn, moving her mouth as if speaking, yet making no sounds. We asked her how she felt now. "When I fell into the swimming pool?" she asked. "I died. I swallowed water. I was yelling for someone to save me." These were the first words Margot had spoken to us directly. Was this a carefully rehearsed drama that she and her sister had put on for our benefit? We found that option difficult to believe. Moreover, the only time Margot had behaved in an ordinary manner was during the trance regression, when her sister had incorporated her purported past life.

"Is it helpful to work together with your sister?" we queried. She looked at us with feigned surprise and replied, "What sister?" She apparently had again taken the role of her past incarnation.

Not Only With Brazilians

We wondered if the mediumship methods of Mendes worked only with Brazilians, who were already culturally predisposed to a belief in spirits. Mendes had invited two of the members of our group, George Araki and Camilla Sherman, to take part in the past life regression session. Mendes commented that both of them appeared to be highly sensitive, and could easily develop their mediumship abilities. They were asked to take part in all the exercises, and then to lie on the floor together with

51

the clinic guests and the other mediums. Araki reported entering into deep relaxation, as if he were drifting or floating in space. Sherman, on the other hand, appeared to be deeply moved during the session, crying through a good part of it. We asked her what she had felt.

"I tried to give myself completely over to it," she commented, "although it wasn't anything that I have done before. I became very dizzy and finally lost consciousness, and when I awakened, I came into semi-consciousness and identified with all of the suffering in the world. It was as if I had become an entity that felt the suffering of humankind. It is hard to describe."

Dr. Mendes is not without adversaries. The Brazilian Medical Association does not permit Mendes to present his work at their meetings. "My work is antipsychiatric," he claims. "It upsets the way that medicine conceptualizes epilepsy. I think that epilepsy has metaphysical elements," Mendes explained, "and is not only a neurological problem as medicine maintains. We have many arguments about this whenever I propose that epilepsy is a bioenergetic and metaphysical phenomenon, while the medical community continues to insist that it is a totally physical one, an illness of the central nervous system. To change their way of thinking is a very difficult task."

Self-Regulation

Once back home, we (Villoldo and Krippner) compared our separate observations of Mendes and his clinic.

I (Villoldo) have seen dozens of epileptics leave Mendes's clinic, some of them after only four weeks of treatment. They appeared to be healed, and did not require any medication or later treatment. At the same time I have observed epileptics leave halfway through the therapy, only to lose all of their gains in a short period of time. It appears to me that for the therapy to be successful, at least one family member must be present. Mendes's professed success rate of 85 percent is based on these two conditions: The epileptic must complete the program, and must be joined by a family member during treatment.

When I directed the Self-Regulation Laboratory at San Francisco State University, we were able to teach our subjects to exercise remarkable control over bodily functions through relaxation and imagery techniques. It is possible that the Umbanda techniques used by Mendes contain powerful instructions for the person to learn to regulate his or her bodily states, particularly the electrical brainstorms associated with epilepsy.

In my (Krippner) discussions with Mendes, I was struck by the likelihood that the treatment encourages a type of self-regulation. All the various types of epilepsy involve dramatic alterations of consciousness, some of them quite spectacular. An epileptic may see auras before a seizure, may have a sense of déjà vu, or may have sensory alterations which indicate that a seizure is about to occur. Through biofeedback, some epileptics have been able to exert some type of control over the episode, thus minimizing the symptoms. Perhaps Mendes's successful clients are doing something similar by shifting their epileptic episode into a mediumistic experience.

During my trip to Rio de Janeiro in 1983, I met with Dr. David Ahkstein, a Brazilian psychiatrist who has also been influenced by the Umbanda rituals. He has developed "Terpsichorean Trance Therapy," named after Terpsichore, the Greek muse of dance. In his Rio office, Ahkstein's clients spin, and then perform a free-style dance to samba music. Basically, it is a type of dance therapy, which appears to be a useful psychotherapeutic adjunct for clients who are anxious, depressed, or suffering from other psychological problems.

I (Villoldo) feel that another example of the Brazilian healers' practical ingenuity would be Mendes's inclusion of a family member in the therapy. This provides encouragement for the clients as well as carryover support once they leave the clinic. Many shamanic practitioners also bring parents, siblings, children, and spouses into the treatment program.

I (Krippner) recall that Albert Schweitzer was aware of the healing value of the "significant friend," and shocked his medical colleagues by allowing a client's family to stay near his hospital in Lambaréné, Gabon, and even do the cooking for the afflicted member of the family. He appears to have been one of the first physicians to acknowledge that modern medicine can gain valuable insights by studying native healing traditions. Mendes has taken this philosophy one step further, actually applying spiritual techniques to conditions such as epilepsy which we consider difficult to cure in the West.

Chapter 4

Drum and Candle Ceremonies: Incorporating the Spirits

Spirit mediumship, spiritist healing, and various forms of exorcism are popular in the Candomblé and Umbanda sects of Brazil. The African slaves who came to Brazil's northeast region, beginning in the 1550s, brought with them from what is today Nigeria, Dahomey, and Cameroon their beliefs about their deities or "Orishas." These powerful, terrifying, and very human gods and goddesses could be talked to, pleaded with, and cajoled through special offerings. Although the slaves were baptized as Christians by the Portuguese colonizers, and forced to attend Roman Catholic mass on Sundays, they continued to practice their native African beliefs. To escape prosecution, they syncretized the Catholic saints and the Orishas, giving the Orishas Christian names. For example, Yemanja, the goddess of the waters, was merged with her Christian counterpart, the Virgin Mary.

Brazil declared its independence in 1822 and the slaves were freed in 1888. By that time, more than fifteen generations of Brazilians had heard the stories of the Orishas, of death by the evil eye, of illness cured by spirit counsel, and of marriages saved by spirit intervention.

The highest echelons of Brazil's upper class nurtured a belief in spirits, fed to them with the milk of their black nurses. Although Brazil is a country of devout Christians, the thoughts and the feelings of the African Orishas still pulsate through its jungles and beaches.

Although the African traditions became divided in Brazil, Candomblé remains the purest form and the one most closely resembling the Yoruba religion of western Africa. Its followers retain the original names of the Yoruba Orishas. In 1830, Brazil's first permanent Candomblé center was organized by three former slaves who became high priestesses, or Mothers of the Saints. The name "Candomblé" probably derived from "candombé," a celebration and dance held by the slaves on coffee plantations. These women trained the Daughters of the Saints in the folklore and magical beliefs of their African ancestors, including incorporation of the various spirit teachers.

Although its origins lie in both the Candomblé and Christian traditions, the Umbanda movement was not founded until 1904. The name "Umbanda" seems to have derived from "Aum-Gandha," a Sanskrit term for the divine principle. Both Umbanda and Candomblé practitioners emphasize the importance of incorporating spirits, and both venerate the figure of Jesus Christ. In Umbanda, the Christian names are generally used for the Orishas rather than the original African ones. While the Mothers of the saints, who operate the Candomblé temple, often return to Africa to be initiated by Yoruba priests, their counterparts in Umbanda, the Fathers and Mothers of the Saints, are initiated and awarded their titles in Brazil. Further, Umbanda syncretized the legacy of the Brazilian Indians with the Yoruba Orishas and the Christian saints of the Portuguese conquerors. Although the rituals of Umbanda and Candomblé vary greatly, they have three beliefs in common. They are:

1. Humans have both a physical and a spiritual body.
2. Disincarnate spirits are in constant contact with the physical world.
3. Humans can learn to incorporate spirits for purposes of healing and evolution.

These beliefs are also shared by Kardec spiritism and by other Afro-Brazilian sects such as Caboclo and Quimbanda.

For many, the philosophies of spiritism, Umbanda, and Candomblé provide greater rewards than does the philosophy of a secular society or a conventional religion. The appeal of becoming a channel for healing is especially strong for those individuals who place great value on a life of service. If students experience spirit incorporation positively, "bringing about sensations of ecstasy and self-transcendence during trance," as a great number of them report, their other needs for personal recognition, for self-development, and for achieving something meaningful and significant in life can be fulfilled.

The Return of Peña Azul

In April 1983, I (Villoldo) led our group to an Umbanda temple in the back of a small suburban home nearly an hour's drive outside the city of São Paulo. We were informed that there would be over two hundred persons attending the ceremony that evening, yet the temple was barely larger than a living room. Half of the temple was filled with chairs arranged in rows, facing an open area where the mediums would gather, which was decorated with figures of Christian saints. On the central wall, above a statue of a Wise Old Black Slave (one of the most important spirit guides of the temple), was a large wall painting of Christ. To its left were three conga drums. The Father of the Saints, dom Roberto, informed us that the "music master" would play the rhythms of each of the spirit guides of the temple on the drums. Both the Yoruba and Christian saints would be called by the rhythm of the drums and by the mediums' songs and chants.

Dom Roberto, a tall congenial man in his early fifties, indicated that we were free to go where we pleased during the ceremony, as we had come dressed in white, the correct color for the evening ritual. He received us as honored guests, and explained that it was permissible for us to walk around the altar and other ritual areas which were ordinarily closed to the public.

Dom Roberto went on to explain that Umbanda sessions are characterized by the incorporation of Indian and African guides as well as the spirits of innocent children who died early in life. In some parts of Brazil, Oriental spirits also make their appearance. However, the major Yoruba Orishas, such as Xango, Ogun, and Oshoshi, are not usually incorporated: The Umbandistas fear that the medium would not be able to endure the intensity involved in such a transaction.

We were totally unprepared for what happened next. One-half hour after our arrival, the temple began to fill with hundreds of people who had come to be treated by the nearly one hundred mediums and healers. There was no room to move, and we were faced with the dilemma of either sitting with the congregation and missing most of the action, or accepting dom Roberto's invitation and joining the multitude of mediums on the floor. We opted for the latter, as we were eager to experience Umbanda mediumship as closely as possible.

The ceremony opened with the mediums singing the songs of the Exus, the Orishas that represent the forces of nature and are thought to be the messengers of the gods. An Exu is also a trickster, and symbolizes the divine unconscious. In his songs he is asked to protect the temple and to prevent any evil from taking place during the evening.

A bottle of cane liquor was placed outside between three candles as an offering for an Exu. Soon after, the Sons and Daughters of the Saints began to sway to the sound of the drums as they sang to Peña Azul, the Indian medicine man who is the chief guide of the temple. Peña Azul enjoys a wide following throughout Brazil, as he was one of the first spirit guides alleged to have worked with the Umbanda mediums. Dom Roberto explained that Peña Azul was a Navaho Indian shaman who died two centuries ago, and who has now returned to heal through the Umbanda mediums.

As the beating of the drums became more frenzied, dom Roberto turned to the painting of Christ over the altar and called upon the spirit of Peña Azul. One could see a tremor running through his body as he incorporated the spirit of the medicine man. Immediately, his assistant brought a blue feather headdress, placed it on the medicine man's head, and handed him a long-stemmed peace pipe of the sort used by North American Indians.

The spirit of Peña Azul began to speak through dom Roberto, saying that he knew the congregation had assembled to receive the gift of healing. He would give this gift to all those present, for they were his spiritual children. He then proceeded to perform a traditional American Indian medicine dance, holding a spear in one hand and the peace pipe in the other, and blessed each member of the congregation, touching their heads lightly with the tip of the lance.

Peña Azul began next to call on the spirits of the Indian medicine men and women to come and take over the bodies of the mediums. He also summoned the spirits of Brazil's jungle shamans and the Wise Old Black Slaves who had perished toiling in the sugar cane plantations. One by one the mediums began to spin and to acquire the postures and mannerisms of the various spirits they were incorporating. For example, the Wise Old Black Slaves appeared to be bent over with age as they were incorporated; the Indians enjoyed smoking large cigars, for tobacco was a sacred plant for the American Indian. Both men and women, as well as some adolescent boys and girls in their mediumship training, could be seen puffing on long cigars, which they smoked throughout the ceremony. The room soon filled with smoke; compounded by the heat of the warm Brazilian evening, the temple became unbearably hot. The mediums, the congregation, and the members of our group were soon drenched in sweat.

After the nearly one hundred mediums had incorporated spirit guides, the members of the congregation came forth to receive healing. For some, the healing consisted of advice concerning their spouses or children, or work; others were diagnosed for physical problems, and herbal and pharmaceutical remedies were prescribed. For others the healing was quite different, consisting of advice to develop their psychic abilities. The *Umbandistas,* like the followers of Candomblé and Kardec spiritism, believe that the most important healing is the healing of the spirit, when one becomes actively engaged in one's spiritual growth.

In one corner we noticed a middle-aged man learning to enter into the ecstatic trance to incorporate the spirit of his guide. He began to pound his chest with both fists in an apelike manner. The mediums explained that the first encounters with the spirits were difficult, and that repressed feelings and emotions had to be released. They interpreted the chest-pounding as an unconscious attempt to open up the various energy centers in the man's body. The mediums explained that he was severely blocked in his heart and solar plexus, the energy centers having to do with feelings, emotions, and the ability to express oneself in the world. Moments later he stopped pounding his chest, and his body began to shake as if he were going into convulsions. The mediums explained that this resulted from the "energy fluids" of the spirit guides as they began to merge with the man's own. According to the *Umbandistas,* in the early stages of mediumship training the initiate's brain is simultaneously inhabited by the two different personalities, causing "energetic changes" in the brain that reverberate throughout the body.

We asked dom Roberto, who was still under the control of Peña Azul, if he would attempt a healing on some of the members of our group. He pointed to George Araki, and indicated that he was ready to take a leap forward in his spiritual growth. Peña Azul said that Dr. Araki needed to have a stronger and more direct connection with his guides, and invited him to the center of the circle. He began to blow smoke in the biologist's face, explaining that he was cleansing the "energy fields" that surrounded his physical body. He then began stimulating Araki's so-called "third eye" located in the forehead; according to Umbanda, this represents the center of consciousness and of one's vision into the spirit world. After a few moments, Dr. Araki began to sway back and forth. At one point he collapsed backward; fortunately two of dom Roberto's assistants were there to catch him.

Dr. Araki later reported, "Umbanda for me was a very warm and calming experience. When the mediums brought me into the circle, with all the frenzy of activity going on around me, and began conducting the ritual, I felt a sensation of surrender: simply giving in, letting go, and trusting. I felt that I was conscious or alert all the way through, but it was just out of the corner of my mind that I had that link with consciousness. Dom Roberto twirled me in such a way that I felt dizzy and then I just collapsed. I felt myself uplifted and surrounded by an energy or force I cannot describe."

Recovering the Soul

The key to Umbanda healings is the ecstatic trance, an altered state of consciousness in which one gains new perspectives on one's psychic capabilities and learns to change the patterns that create illness for ones that create health.[1] The songs of Umbanda reaffirm the healing message that the spirit never dies but continues on its eternal journey in other worlds. The most enlightened spirits choose to come back to teach and heal through the mediums of Umbanda. For the followers of this syncretic religion, mediumship establishes a connection with these evolved minds, a link that, in the beliefs of Umbanda, elevates the medium to ever higher plateaus of consciousness.[2]

In the Umbanda session we attended, the spirit of Peña Azul spoke in a language that none of us understood. His words had to be translated by one of the other healers, who claimed that this was an ancient American Indian dialect. Peña Azul motioned to another one of our group's members, Edmundo Barbosa, a Brazilian clinical psychologist. Through the translator, he explained that Barbosa was under the influence of subtle yet powerful forces that could eventually result in serious illness. He explained that Barbosa should undergo a ritual of symbolic death, during which he would journey to the world of the spirits to "recover his soul" and regain his health. He instructed the psychologist to lie on the floor and covered him with a white cloth. The medicine man began to dance around him, shaking his rattle and thrusting his spear over Barbosa's heart. The rhythm of the drums had changed, becoming more acute and piercing.

Peña Azul then began to thrust his spear in the direction of Barbosa's head. Suddenly he knelt down and began to gesture with a knife, as if he were cutting open the psychologist's chest. According to one of the assistants, this represented the death of the physical body and purportedly launched his spirit on a journey to the other world.

Peña Azul then took a candle and moved it in circles over each of Barbosa's "energy centers," from the top of the head to the lower belly. One of the healers explained to us that during the death ceremony old sorrows from the past, which are often the cause of illness, are allowed to die. They are symbolically left behind in the underworld, from which the spirit returns cleansed.

Afterward, we asked Barbosa what he felt during the ritual. He replied, "At the beginning I felt tense and uncomfortable and then I decided to just close my eyes and let it happen. Once I made that decision, I began to feel an opening in my body as if I were being torn apart. This was followed by a sensation of power and I realized that I had made contact with something in me, something protecting me. Afterwards I regretted that it had finished so soon. I felt a great relief afterwards. I felt at least ten or twenty pounds lighter than before."

By now it was past midnight and time for the ceremony to come to an end. Peña Azul turned to the congregation and observed that the heart of the world today was very dark. The world was in great crisis, he said, and many people were concerned about the possibility of the Earth's being destroyed. Yet, the medicine man predicted, "In a short while, the world will begin to change and to improve. Think of me and I will be with you." He exhorted the congregation to take part in the healing of the planet, through whatever line of work or occupation one had. The medicine man performed a closing dance, blessed the congregation, and returned dom Roberto to his body. Dom Roberto gave us a warm farewell as we left the temple and emerged into the cool Brazilian night.

The Spirits of Candomblé

In April 1983, I (Villoldo) led a group which visited the Candomblé temple of Yemanja, located in a small town outside the city of Recife. The temple is situated next to a Roman Catholic cathedral. Both are located on top of a small hill with a sweeping view of the bay and the city. Pãe (father) Edu, the head of the temple, commented on the irony that more townspeople attend his temple than the Catholic cathedral.

Life-size sculptures of the Orishas lined the temple walls, with Yemanja, the goddess of the waters and patroness of the temple, appearing as a sensual young woman in a clinging, low-cut dress. On the other end of the temple was the statue of an Exu, a messenger of the gods corresponding to the Roman god Mercury and the Greek Hermes. The Christian priests mistakenly identified the Exus as the devil, as they are often represented with horns and dressed in red and black. Pãe Edu explained that these Orishas represent the unconscious forces at work inside all of us. These forces must be respected and acknowledged; otherwise they appear as fears, doubts, and acts of self-destruction. Exu as an individual is a benevolent trickster and is responsible for the mischief in the world.

The Father of the Saints invited the group to a ceremony of initiation which would take place in the temple that evening. A young man who had fasted for more than ten days was to have his first contact with the Orishas.

That evening, there were over fifty male and female mediums in the room. They were dressed in brightly colored garments similar to those used in Carnaval. (In fact,

Carnaval originated in part from the festivities of Candomblé.) Pãe Edu signaled for the drummers to begin playing, and the dancers formed a circle around him, moving rhythmically in a counterclockwise direction. They opened the ceremony with the song of Yemanja. Next, a woman and a man dressed in long red robes appeared. They represented the African kings and queens in the dancers' reenactment of the painful exodus from Africa and the voyage to the New World. The dancers then pushed a wooden ship nearly fifteen feet long into the room. Instead of the cramped Portuguese slave ships, this was a modern ocean liner decorated with flowers and bearing a young girl. She wore a long blue robe and a crown in the shape of a half moon, the symbol of Yemanja. This ritual is a vindication of history—a glorious recreation of the ignominious journey in the slave ships. Through the songs and dances, the people remember that it was the Africans who were the real conquerors of the New World. It was they who built the roads, cultivated the cotton and sugar plantations, and built the cities that brought greatness to both North and South America.

The dancers began to call on the Exus, who represent the primal force of all life and nature. They offered the Exus a strong cane liquor inside a clay vessel, and asked them to safeguard the temple, especially on this night of initiation. As Pãe Edu brought the liquor to the statue of Exu, the dancers gestured with their hands to expel all evil from the house. The dancers stopped when Pãe Edu appeared holding a black pigeon, which he passed over everyone's body, symbolically cleansing all the participants in preparation for the ceremony of initiation. He took the pigeon before the statue of the trickster, twisted its head off, and left it to bleed on a stone at the feet of an Exu, a sight found revolting by many of us.

The dancers changed into white clothing, and arranged

fruits, liquor, flowers, and fish along a path leading from the center of the room to a floor-level throne. At the other end of the pathway, facing the throne, was a stool with a wicker basket. Edu explained that the spirits must first be consulted to see if Jose Arnaldo, the initiate, was truly prepared for the initiation. He said that he must also consult the Orishas to see if they approved of our filming procedures. To do this, Pãe Edu shook the *busios*, the seashells through which destiny speaks, onto the wicker basket. The arrangement of the shells was examined and it was determined that the signs were favorable for the young man. In addition, we were invited to stay. The shells also said that Jose Arnaldo was ready to receive the spirit of Ogun, the warrior god, and that the ceremony could proceed. (Unlike the Umbanda temple we visited earlier, this congregation had no hesitation about incorporating the more powerful Orishas.)

The young man was brought in by the Mother of the Saints, a woman with skin black as coal. She had received her training and initiation in Africa from priests who carry on the original traditions that were imported to Brazil with the slaves. (While Pãe Edu was the political head of the temple, the Mother of the Saints was the spiritual head and led all the esoteric ceremonies. Originally, Candomblé offices were restricted to women; today, when male mediums do attain a key role, it is usually political rather than spiritual in nature.)

The dancers sat facing each other in two rows, with Pãe Edu and the Mother of the Saints at one end, and Jose Arnaldo sitting on the throne at the other end. Pãe Edu asked that the initiate develop wings to fly into the spirit world and that he be protected from his enemies and from the psychological traps of life. Most important, he asked that Jose Arnaldo realize the eternity of the spirit. In his prayers, Pãe Edu explained that the slave was master of his life in a way that even the European conquerors were not, for the African was not afraid to die. The freedom that the slaves had lost in the physical world they found in the world of the spirit.

One by one the dancers stood up and brought an offering of fruit or fish that they had cultivated or caught, touching it to the head of the young man. (The *ori*, or head, is where the spirit of the Orisha is thought to reside after initiation.) Next, Pãe Edu and the Mother of the Saints began to chant, singing, "The priests of this house are asking you, great gods of Africa, to join us. Our gods were denied by the Christian church because it was a sect of the black people. We call on you now to come, oh gods from black Africa!"

In the initiatory ritual, Jose Arnaldo would be possessed by the spirit of Ogun. There were dangers during an initiation of this sort, as the psyche might not be able to tolerate the intensity of the contact with an Orisha. To safeguard against this, Pãe Edu ate black peppercorns from Africa, asking that the initiate acquire strength from the earth. Next, two white pigeons were passed over the boy's body to purify him. One of the pigeons was brought to Pãe Edu, who prayed that the encounter with the Orisha be gentle. The first incorporation of an Orisha is often shocking and violent; thus the Orisha is asked to take the head of the pigeon and its blood and to have mercy on the head of the young initiate. Pãe Edu twisted off the head of the white pigeon, which the Mother of the Saints placed on the head of Jose Arnaldo. Yellow cornmeal that had been pressed into a small cake was placed on the youth's head so that he would have the strength to work and the courage to be proud of his past.

Pãe Edu, the Mother of the Saints, and all the mediums of the temple brought their heads down to the floor to await the coming of Ogun, the warrior god. A few moments later, the young man began to shake. Ogun had arrived and the congregation broke into song. One by one, all the members of the temple came up to pay their respects to Ogun, who now occupied the body and mind of the young man. They bowed before the initiate, paying their respects to the living god.

It was difficult for the young man to tolerate the intensity of the divinity and he had to be helped to his feet by two men. He was led outside and shown the night sky, as this was the last time he would see the stars for forty days. After the initiation was finished, he would remain in meditation in a small room inside the temple until his union with Ogun was complete. During his meditations, he needed to acquire the strength of the warrior and the vision to meet the gods face to face. The mediums believed that the spirit of Ogun would transform the young man's body and that he would acquire a double life, inhabiting both the Earth and the life of the spirit world.

The Afro-Brazilian spiritual traditions speak of the importance of healing the spirit, and Brazilian Candomblé carries on this belief in the New World. The followers of Candomblé believe that the greatest healing occurs during initiation, when an individual becomes one with the god. Some outsiders consider the Candomblé rites to be primitive, but the followers of Candomblé point out that some Western religious practices seem barbaric, such as when the "body of Christ" is eaten during Christian communion services. It is much more sublime, they say, to offer your body and mind to be inhabited by the gods.

Villoldo's experiences with Umbanda and Candomblé were very much like mine (Krippner). When I visited the city of Salvador in 1983, there were three branches of Candomblé and over three hundred temples in Salvador and the state of Bahia alone. Many of the temples allow only women to be mediums, and they honor the original African deities such as Yemanja, Ogun, and Obatala, rather than their Christian equivalents. Again, there are exceptions, with Christ taking a place of honor in most temples.

In the city of Salvador, I visited the historic Casa Branca ("White House") and spoke with Mãe ("mother") Meninhina de Gantois, whose grandmother had led a secession from the original Candomblé group a century earlier. She recalled, "Grandmother could look at a person and give a whole life story. I cannot do this because I am only the granddaughter." Mãe Meninhina's grandfather was not enthusiastic about his wife's devotion to the spirits. He asked why had he been permitted to become a slave, if they were as powerful as she claimed. Nor was Mãe Meninhina's father pleased when she herself was called, in dreams and visions, to become a medium. She feels that her father's objection to her initiation was the reason why he died a cripple. According to Mãe Meninhina, when the spirits call, there is no other path to take. If you spurn or ignore the call, you may become physically or mentally disturbed.

In Africa, sacred rituals were primarily a male prerogative. In Brazil, however, male slaves were preoccupied with their labors in the field, and ceremonial duties often fell to the women. A number of slave women gained stature by becoming the concubines of their Portuguese masters, and claimed that the practice of their African rites was necessary to maintain their sexual prowess. The freed female slaves who founded the first temple of Candomblé saw to it that men were excluded from major responsibility, although they were allowed to serve as assistants and to play the drums during the rituals. This may have been another reason why Mãe Meninhina's grandfather and father were not enthusiastic members of the sect.

I was able to contrast Candomblé with Umbanda in 1983 when our group visited an Umbanda temple in Rio de Janeiro and we all volunteered for healings. In my case, the medium announced that I had picked up a "low river spirit" upon my arrival, and that it needed to be exorcised. I was quite willing, and dutifully fell backward just like the others I had observed. However, I was quite surprised at the feeling of dissociation and disorientation I experienced following the exorcism. It took me half an hour to regain my composure so that I could walk up to the Mother of the Saints for my final blessing.

The Brazilian mediums generally speak of "lower" spirits or "mischievous" spirits instead of "evil" spirits. They see all consciousness as a pattern of evolution, and the spirits who have done wrong simply need to be educated. But whether one thinks of the spirits as disincarnate entities or as subpersonalities, they are associated with the release of considerable unconscious material. A medium can act out—or incorporate—spirits of the opposite sex, of different ages, and of various ethnic groups, allowing repressed areas of the psyche to find expression.

Both of us (Villoldo and Krippner) have noticed that the theme of self-regulation runs through these mediumistic sessions as well. It takes considerable training for a medium to enter a profound altered state of consciousness and engage in spirit incorporation. Mediums seem to have mastered the art of putting their everyday selves aside, of standing out of their own way.

Some people may perform better as healers after entering an altered state. They are able to leave their ordinary beliefs and behaviors behind, assuming new roles and identities that might give them the confidence to evoke the self-healing capacities of their patients.

The ability to abandon ordinary worldviews for new, health-supporting ones may be an essential element of the healing process that we can learn from the trance healers. Whereas allopathic physicians treat the illness and return the patient to unhealthy habits and environments, the practitioners of Candomblé and Umbanda claim that this is not sufficient. They believe that healing is the result of one's lifestyle, and claim healing is not complete until one also "heals" the relationship with one's spouse, children, parents, and work. They claim that disease arises not only from organic malfunctions but also because of the way one relates to God, the Earth, oneself, and one's fellow humans. For healing to be complete, all of these relationships must be brought into harmony; then the body can not help but make a healthy response.

Chapter 5

The Buddhist Firewalkers

Every year members of the Kanon Buddhist temple in the outskirts of São Paulo commemorate the birth of the Buddha with the feast of Hai Watari, the walking over fire. Though this ceremony of healing and transformation was once a secret ritual, the monks believe that it can no longer be kept behind the monastery walls because the world is in great need of healing. For more than twenty years they have invited the local community to participate.

The monks are descendants of the Japanese settlers who came to the New World in search of a better life at the turn of this century. When they built the original pagoda-like temple nearly sixty years ago, the village of Ipiranga was an agricultural community, and they were among its first settlers. Today, São Paulo, the third largest city in the world, with nearly seventeen million inhabitants, has swallowed up the once rural community. Still, the temple exists in relative anonymity, for Brazil is a country that tolerates many faiths and forms of religious practice.

I (Villoldo) took our group of researchers to the temple, arriving in the early morning, for it had been announced that there were certain preparations that all who wanted to walk over the burning coals had to undergo. Although the firewalk itself would not take place until late that evening, the temple was filled to capacity. We had arrived in time for the first service, and found Siba, the head monk, at the altar with his back turned to the congregation. He was rhythmically striking a bright red wooden instrument shaped like a gourd which produced a tone that reverberated throughout the hall. The altar itself was filled with flowers and fruits as an offering to the Buddha and to the goddess Kanon, the guardian of the temple. We later found out that Kanon was the goddess of compassion and represented the creative forces in the universe; according to mythology, she was born from the original fires of creation itself.

Toward the end of the service a single file of people stepped to the altar, to a bowl surrounded by flowers and filled with water. In the center of the bowl stood a small statue of the Buddha, over which each person poured three ladles of the colored liquid. As the congregation paid their respects to the Buddha, they were reminded that the Buddha was not God, but represented a state of enlightenment that is attainable by every individual.

Arrival of the Dragon

At three o'clock that afternoon a procession led by the eldest monks and ending with the youngest children moved to the temple grounds for the lighting of the fire. In the center of the grounds we found a neatly stacked woodpile nearly seven feet high, three feet wide, and over fifteen feet long. It had been stacked at six o'clock that morning to capture the rising sun's first rays. First the monks and then the youngest children saluted the woodpile, and made an offering of steamed rice to the Earth.

Siba, the head monk, said it was difficult to explain the

meaning of the fire ceremony. "We are going to walk over the coals," he said, "but not on them. In the beginning, before the Earth was created, the goddess Kanon would travel through the heavens on the back of a dragon, who represents all of the forces of nature. We are going to pray to the goddess Kanon, who will come with her dragon and lie over the coals, so that we can walk over the dragon's back. That's how our feet do not get burned." We asked Siba how he knew when the dragon had arrived. Smiling, he said, "There are so many things that people would like to know. I have been working in the temple for thirty years, but there is so little that I can explain." The monk said that fire was the transforming element in nature, and that it would purify and heal us as we walked across during the ritual.

Before lighting the fire, four young monks with lances advanced to the woodpile to salute the four corners of the Earth, calling on the spirits of the North, West, South, and East, and all the forces of nature. Then, with torches that were lit from the candles on the altar, they proceeded to light the fire.

Inside the temple, the priests continued the service for those townspeople who would walk over the red-hot coals. The preparatory rite consisted of placing a piece of wood with one's name written on it into a small fire that burned in a sandbox above which hung papier-mâché banners. Siba explained that this fire symbolized the pyre that Buddhists use to cremate the bodies of their dead, and symbolically burns away the false persona or mask behind which the Buddhists believe our true nature lies.

The monks claim that great healing benefits are derived from the fire ritual, but that it does not always result in the alleviation of symptoms, as in our Western healing practices. The Buddhists are interested in treating the spiritual causes of illness (and not only offering symptomatic relief), for it is their belief that disease results when one becomes estranged from God. During the fire ceremony the sick as well as the healthy are reminded that the Fire of Heaven burns within them, and that the goal of healing is to discover one's spiritual nature.

By four o'clock the fire was burning vigorously, with flames leaping fifteen feet into the air. Four young monks with lances aimed approached the fire and began to symbolically tame Kanon's dragon, alternately thrusting with their lances and bowing respectfully to the fire. This procedure was repeated by a number of monks, as the ritual also served as an opportunity for the young men to learn to tame the fires of their passions.

Two hours later the fire was reduced to a bed of burning coals which two monks spread out into a rectangle twenty feet long and ten feet wide. The Buddhists allowed us to observe the ritual from within the fire area, where normally only the monks are allowed in order to tend the fire. From this vantage point, we were able to follow closely all the steps of the ritual, while feeling the nearly unbearable blast of heat from the fire. We observed that the monks always walked in a clockwise direction around the fire, as they said this was the direction in which everything in the universe moved, from the galaxies and solar systems to the spiral of the chambered nautilus.

Around seven o'clock in the evening, the head monk changed from the orange robes of the priest to the plain white robes of the peasant, for he had to cross the fire as a common person. He bowed by the four sides of the fire pit, greeted the dragon and the goddess Kanon, and prayed that this would become a holy fire, for the Buddhist traditions hold that only after the dragon lies on the coals can one walk safely over them. He then poured saki onto the coals as an offering to the dragon, and we could see the alcohol vaporize as it touched the coals.

The time had come for the priest to test the fire. Siba took a ceremonial spear, for the forces of nature had to be met with courage, in the spirit of the warrior. By now over three hundred people had gathered on the grounds, and the crowd became silent as the monk walked to the end of the fire pit, and with a samurai scream charged through the burning coals.

The Buddhists claim that our beliefs limit our experience, and that we cannot usually walk over fire because we believe that the task is impossible. Our beliefs were soon put to the test.

Siba invited those who had taken part in the preparatory ceremony in the temple to walk across the fire pit, and gestured for our group to go first. We looked at each other in disbelief, wondering if we would go through with it or not. Since I was the leader, the group felt I should be the first one to proceed. With all the courage I could muster, I walked to the fire pit, where a smiling Siba said, "It's a friendly dragon, my friend. Do not be afraid." I took a step into the six-inch-deep bed of coals, and realized to my horror that I was in the middle of a fiery inferno, and with all my strength leapt back to safety. Walking barefoot through burning coals ran against every ounce of common sense I had in me. Yet at the same time I realized I might never again have this opportunity. I braced myself and walked the seven steps that it took to cross the fire pit, and halfway through experienced a sensation of tranquility that I have never felt before or since. For although I could feel intense heat in all of my body, my feet remained cool and unburned.

The Healing Fire

The monks believe that if one is suffering from an illness, one will have a pin burn on the foot—on the acupuncture point that corresponds to the affected organ. The fire supposedly burns the illness out through the acupuncture point. Several members of our group were suffering from kidney and intestinal problems, as we had just come from a physically exhausting three weeks in the desert and jungles of Peru. I had a case of inflamed kidneys that had been bothering me for over a week. After crossing the fire, I found that I had a pin burn on my left foot that supposedly coincided with the kidney acupuncture point. Within three days my kidney condition had improved.

The monks heard that there were several scientists in the group who, to satisfy their scientific curiosity, wanted to be the first to walk through the pit before the coals were trampled under by the several hundred pairs of feet that were to follow. Our group members had the opportunity to walk through the coals several times. Daniel Gunther, a medical doctor, commented: "I really aimed for some very hot red ones. The last step that I took produced a small burn on my left foot, but it was very small, and it did not hurt at all after a few seconds. Other than that, there was no pain at all. I could feel the coals moving under my feet and I could feel warmth, but not intense heat and no pain." He went on to say, "All of a sudden my sense of the possible, my entire framework for how I view the world, changed, and it was not when I walked over the coals, but when I decided to do it—when I took my shoes off, rolled up my pants, and knew that I was going to walk across."

Another member of the group, Camilla Sherman, a musician, captured the flavor of our experience when she said, "I never for a moment disbelieved that this would be possible for people to do, but I never believed it would be possible for me to do."

Several hundred members of the local community—farmers, mechanics, bus drivers, and factory workers—had come for the firewalking ritual. One man claimed that he had participated for over ten years, and that the ceremony had transformed his life, eliminating a serious chronic illness and helping to cure his wife of a drinking problem. Others had come only for the drama of the occasion, and stood by the sidelines watching. The monks believe that even if one does not participate in the ritual there are healing effects, the most important being a demonstration that we have capabilities and powers we do not even suspect. The Buddhists claim that when consciousness is awakened, one can walk over fire. They also say that there are few limits to what the person with an awakened mind can do.

One member of our group, George Araki, claimed that he did not know what to expect when the monks invited him to walk across the fire pit. "I had thoughts," he said, "that perhaps this would even be the end of me." When we asked what kind of explanation he had for being able to walk through the bed of hot coals, he said, "I don't have a scientific explanation. I don't even want to develop one at this point. I think what is important is that science can only deal with a certain realm of phenomena. This is a real phenomenon that occurred, but which science cannot fully explain at this time."

We had brought a laboratory thermometer that registered 680°F (350°C), a temperature at which human flesh is charred. The measurements were taken at the end of the ceremony, nearly six hours after the fire had been lit, when many of the coals had been reduced to dying embers. In all probability, the temperature in the middle of the pit was much hotter, particularly before the public was allowed to walk. With their extraordinary firewalking demonstration, the Buddhists may not be far from the truth when they say that we are able to transcend our limitations and tap the unchartered realm of spiritual possibilities.

Firewalking in Other Cultures

Brazil is not the only country where firewalking is attempted. There are yearly festivals in Sri Lanka and Singapore, and similar religious rituals in Japan, Greece, India, Spain, Thailand, Fiji, and other places. When I (Krippner) was in Bulgaria, I was told that firewalking had become a discipline for a number of young people who wanted to demonstrate that Marxist atheists could firewalk just as well as the mountain people who have attributed their success to religious faith.

Firewalking phenomena date back to the earliest recorded history. Pliny the Elder wrote of an ancient Roman family, the Harpi, who proudly walked over a charred pile of logs at the yearly festival of Apollo. A group of firewalkers from Kosti, Greece, yearly commemorate the legend of St. Constantine, who is said to have walked into a burning church in 1250 to save the sacred icons. In the Vedic hymns, a tale is told of forcing accused persons to walk over fire to establish their innocence.

The most frequently cited explanation of firewalking states that the primary protection of one's feet comes from the natural moisture in them. A thin layer of perspiration, partially vaporizing at a high temperature, provides protection in accordance with the Leidenfrost principle. (This is the principle which explains why drops of water "dance" above a hot plate for some time before boiling off.) However, this explanation cannot account for those firewalkers who claim to stand or kneel in the hot coals for several minutes, if their claims are valid.

Nor can it explain why some people walk the fire safely, and others who walk at the same time get badly burned.[1] The latter phenomenon indicates that individual differences, both physical and psychological, may play an important role in the effect.

It is likely that several different mechanisms might be at play. Sweat, dirt, and other types of insulation provide protection. Changes in blood circulation might help conduct heat away from body surfaces or reduce the flow of heat to vulnerable tissues. Changes in the functioning of local nerves might suppress the activity of neurochemicals that mediate pain and inflammatory reaction to strong stimulation. In addition, there is the possibility of some unusual capacity of the nervous system to absorb potentially harmful forms of energy, transform them, and conduct them away from the body surface. In any event, firewalking may demonstrate, at least in part, a type of self-regulation which, once explained, may have implications for body-mind relationships and applications to self-healing.

Firewalking in California

Firewalking has taken root in the United States in recent years, most prominently in California. One teacher, Tolly Burkhan, claims to have taught over seven thousand people to walk over burning coals. His preparatory exercises include signing a release form which waives legal responsibility in case of injury, expression of motives by all participants, group singing, and group discussions while everyone takes part in the building of the fire. Burkhan tells his students:

"When you face fire, you will go through fear, much fear. When you decide that you can walk, that you are able to make the first step, this transformation will occur in your body. Therefore, if you can take this first step,

step on the coals and keep walking. You will feel heat, strong heat, but nothing more than that, like walking on hot sand. Do not stop, just keep walking.''[2]

After the three-hour preparation, Burkhan begins the ceremony. Everyone is given an opportunity, but those who do not walk are under no pressure to do so. (Also, some people claim to have firewalked successfully without Burkhan's preparation—or the fees required.) Afterward, for those who have made the walk, he states:

"Fire was a model. If you walked on fire you will be able to overcome fear in your life. There will be many other situations in your life when you will experience fear, but it will not stop you from action."[3] Burkhan uses the word "heat" advisedly. Temperature differs from heat, and porous embers will not conduct heat as efficiently as, say, a sheet of metal, even though the temperature is identical.

According to those who have taken measurements, the coals at Burkhan's ceremonies average 1,300°F (700°C). He claims to have learned the feat from a friend who studied with Tibetan monks. The immunity to cold among Tibetans was documented by Herbert Benson, who has investigated Buddhist monks who were able to raise their skin temperature in icy environments beyond any capacity previously recorded.[4] Fire immunity needs the same type of rigorous study that Benson applied to his study of Tibetans.

PART II

A Journey of Initiation

$\mathbb{I}$n this section you will observe what takes place when a small group of people from several parts of the world embark on a series of initiatory experiences with a well-known Peruvian shaman, don Eduardo Calderon. These apprentices are led through healing ceremonies in natural settings, sacred temples, and archeological sites including Machu Picchu, the ancient Incan spiritual retreat. Shamanism is not an institutionalized religion; rather, it is an attitude, a discipline, and a state of mind that emphasizes the loving care and concern of oneself, one's family, one's community, and one's environment.

You will notice the emphasis that shamans place upon protecting Mother Earth and will ponder how to follow this example. We live in an age of acid rain, pollution, erosion, oil spills, overpopulation, famine, the Love Canal, the Chernobyl accident, and the rupture of the ozone layer. In the 1980s, Americans annually disposed of 350 billion tons of garbage and sewage, one billion tons of mining wastes, 50 billion metal cans, 20 million tons of paper, and 7 million wornout automobiles, and have poured 140 million tons of smoke and noxious fumes into the air we breathe. Since 1950, two-thirds of Central America's rain forests have been slashed and burned. Around the world, at least 10,000 people die each week of starvation, and more than half the earth's people are undernourished by medical standards.

There are any number of ways that shamanic consciousness can permeate your life. "Household Ecology" is an attempt to reduce waste and pollution on a house-by-house basis by educating homemakers, and

85

"Organic Gardening" fosters ways of growing flowers, fruits, and vegetables that enhance the soil rather than depleting and poisoning it. There are designated locations in most communities where you can leave waste paper and metal for recycling. The proceeds of many musical cassettes and records are being donated to fight starvation. A San Francisco financial service firm, Working Assets, has begun marketing a Visa credit card that shares some of its revenues with groups working for peace and environmental protection. A Baltimore investment firm, the Calvert Fund, has established a portfolio of stocks in companies that work actively on behalf of preserving ecology and ending hunger.

Part of Brazil's sugar cane crop goes into the production of "gasohol" which now provides half of the country's automotive power requirements. The Amazonian copaiba tree may be able to produce a fuel that can be used for diesel-powered cars. Alternatives to harmful herbicides, insulating equipment, and packaging materials are utilized in Scandinavia and other ecologically minded areas of the world. Homes are being built that rely heavily on solar or wind power, reducing dependence on fossil fuels and atomic energy.

Don Eduardo has been accused of betraying his Native American heritage by revealing the knowledge of shamanism to outsiders. His critics claim that the Western conquerors who stole the Indian's lands and customs are now, in a modern guise, stealing their sacred rituals and beliefs. Don Eduardo replies that there is precious little time to develop an ecological and spiritual awareness of the earth as our Mother. He insists that the uncontrolled movement toward nuclear destruction and ecological annihilation must be met with an equal movement toward honoring all life on the planet and becoming caretakers of the earth.

Chapter 6

The Shaman's Journey

For many years, I (Villoldo) have traveled to South America to study the healing practices of native American medicine men and women. The healers I met explained that healing occurs within the social context of the community, and felt that when a person was sick, the entire community was afflicted. Sometimes for the healing process to be effective, members of the family and community have to be present; if nothing else, peer pressure helps to remind the sick person that he or she has embarked on a path of self-healing. While researching Eduardo Calderon Palomino's healing methods between 1970 and 1979, I gradually found myself becoming a student of the shaman. After more than ten years of study with don Eduardo, I asked the Peruvian healer for permission to bring a small group of people to Peru to learn the shaman's steps of initiation into the world of the spirit. Don Eduardo agreed, for in a vision he had been told that it was important to reveal his knowledge of healing and shamanism to outsiders. Don Eduardo believes that as the American Indian peoples are diminishing in number, their ranks need to be augmented with other shamans, the new caretakers of the Earth.[1]

I invited a select group from various countries of the

world to make up a global tribe to take through the traditional steps of shamanic initiation. In March of 1983 our group came together in Paracas Bay, two hundred miles south of Lima, Peru. There were twelve of us from five different countries, making up a global tribe that over the next three weeks would undergo the tests and trials to learn what don Eduardo claimed were the first steps to becoming a "person of knowledge." Our members included, among others, an American solar energy specialist, two West German medical doctors, a filmmaker from Munich, a computer analyst from New York, an Austrian architect, a Spanish management consultant, and an American engineer.

The Giant Candelabra

Our group met for the first time in a small hotel on the tropical waters of Paracas Bay. The following day we were to visit the giant Candelabra of Paracas, a figure of unknown origin, nearly three hundred feet in length, which is carved into the side of a ridge that rises straight up out of the water. The figure is shaped like a giant candelabra or tree of life, which to shamans of the area represents a map to the discovery of shamanic knowledge. The shamans believe it is a power center that captures and radiates the energy of the cosmos. For centuries, shamans' apprentices have come here to pray for a vision and to observe alterations in the structure as possible predictions of earthquakes and other changes in the earth.

Early the following morning, we hired two boats to take us to the giant figure. The pilots were reluctant to land their craft, for the area was surrounded by steep cliffs save for a diminutive inlet where six-foot waves washed over the rocky beach. From the beach it was only a short climb to the figure. We had been told to enter from the base and hike up the middle branch of the tree of life. Don Eduardo instructed us to sit along the base of the triangle halfway up the figure and enter into meditation.

As we took our places along the two-hundred-foot-long base of the triangle, the shaman asked Martin, a West German medical doctor, to sit at the far right of the figure on the corner representing the body, and asked me to sit at the far left, on the corner representing the mind, while don Eduardo sat at the top, the corner representing the spirit. By now it was ten in the morning and the sun was scorching our backs. Yet, as soon as the meditation began we forgot about the heat and attempted to appreciate the power of this figure. The shaman began to chant, calling on the spirits of the Earth and the Sun and asking that we each discover a transforming vision that would give greater personal meaning to our journey. Don Eduardo explained that a true vision comes rarely, and must be renewed, reaffirmed, and cared for like a precious sapling, so that it grows strong within us.

After the meditation we returned to the base of the mountain. The shaman told us he had seen a Christ-like figure holding two worlds in his hands, one positive and one negative, and bringing balance between the two. He explained that one of the shaman's roles is to bring balance to the world. As his students, we had to acquire knowledge of both the forces of the light and the forces of the dark and learn to bring them into harmony. If we were to become polarized toward either the light or the dark we would become trapped by that aspect of reality and our spiritual development would be crippled.

What don Eduardo said agreed with my observations of the practices of malevolent practitioners: their techniques for carrying out "black magic" or sorcery are virtually identical to the techniques used by the shamanic healer. Similar rituals and power objects are used by both. The principal difference between the shaman and the sorcerer is that the former has a more highly developed sense of ethics than the malevolent practitioner. I explained to don Eduardo that our doctors have to undergo intensive training for many years in medical school, where they learn about pharmaceutical remedies, the human body, and specialized techniques such as surgery and diagnosis. Many times don Eduardo responded with the question, "In the training of your healers, what steps do they take to attune with the Mother Earth and with the Great Spirit?" I said that how one worshipped was left entirely in the hands of the individual, but that the pressures of medical school often left little time for anything other than one's studies. Don Eduardo was incredulous that our healers spent so much time learning "techniques" and hardly any time in the developing of healing ethics and spiritual values! In his tradition, people who ignore the spirit and concern themselves only with technique are considered sorcerers.*

While at the base of the giant Candelabra, don Eduardo said that the time for sharing our visions would come on the desert, sixty kilometers south of the Candelabra, which we would visit the following day. He felt that his own vision was a positive omen, a sign that we could continue on our path, as we had been welcomed by the nature spirits who were the guardians of these sacred places.

Later that evening, don Eduardo explained that if he had received a bad omen in his vision, we would have had to stop our journey of initiation. I mentioned that these people had come from Europe and North America and that we could not simply tell them to go back home!

---

* I would later learn that the worst kind of sorcery is that which one directs against oneself, contributing to what we call psychosomatic disease, stress-related ills, and some of the medically incurable cancers.

He replied that there were no guarantees on a quest such as this and that the effort we invested was no greater than that of a young Indian who came by foot from a distant village to reenact this journey.

That evening we held the first of our nightly tribal meetings. "We must begin to think of ourselves as a tribe," I explained as we opened the meeting. "This is the first time an international tribe has come together to be admitted into the knowledge of Peruvian shamanism." I explained that don Eduardo had agreed to accept the group as his apprentices for the next three weeks. It was possible that none, or only a few, would complete the steps necessary to become healers and neophyte shamans. Only within the synergism of a tribe could we hope to understand the healing and spiritual practices of this South American Indian shaman.

When we had gathered again that evening, each person explained what motivated him to come on this journey. I asked, "What reasons brought you here? This is of the greatest importance because we must develop a sense of group purpose for our tribe."

Uta explained she was a *heilpractiker* (a naturopathic doctor) in West Germany, and wanted to integrate the healing practices of shamanism with her previous medical training. Carol, a computer analyst from New York, reported that she had come to learn as much as she could about spiritual healing. For her it was important to unify the wisdom of the intellect with the body. Eva, an Austrian architect, felt that she had accidentally performed sorcery on an acquaintance who had a serious accident after they ended an argument. "I didn't know what I was doing," she said. "I think it is very important for me to learn more about myself, about my energy and my power. I need to learn how to handle my power, otherwise my power will be handling me." Clara, a Spanish management consultant, said, "I had a very strong call to come here. I could not avoid it. I think the purpose was for me to find the energies that will help me to heal myself in order to help heal the group of people that I contact in everyday life.''

After everyone shared his or her reason for joining our tribe, don Eduardo nodded in approval. He explained that although this was the first time he had met us in person, he had previously contacted each one of us in his dreams. He said we should pay careful attention to our dreams that evening, for the vision that had begun to incubate in our meditation at the Candelabra would grow and eventually begin to "dream us," as dreams are the medicine person's window into the spirit world. "This vision grows inside you and comes forth in all of your work," he explained. "While the first duty of the medicine man or woman is to heal the sick, he or she is also responsible for the healing of the planet. The most important requirement is to develop your will and to use your power, discovering your spiritual strengths and bringing them forth into the world.''

The Place of the Power Animals

At six o'clock the following morning we left Paracas Bay for a three-hour ride to the *altiplano,* the high plateaus of Nazca. In an area covering over two hundred square miles, one can see gigantic figures of birds, fish, reptiles, and mile-long lines and rectangles carved into the desert floor. No one is certain of the exact origin of these figures or who the original builders were. To the shaman this is the place of the power animals, each animal representing an aspect of power and wisdom that a shaman must develop. For centuries shamans brought their apprentices here to acquire the devotion of the pelican (which in times of scarcity will feed its young with its own flesh), the endurance of the hummingbird, the speed and agility of the cougar, the patience of the spider, and the vision of the eagle. According to the legends, it is also a place of cleansing and purification, where one can release past sorrows and pains.

Before visiting the desert figures, we met with Professor Josue Lancho, the foremost Peruvian authority on the giant hieroglyphs. Professor Lancho explained that the figures predated Incan times, and many were over fifteen hundred years old, presumably built by the Nazca Indians who had settled near this site. He noted that the markings were first seen from the air in 1927. Archeologists thought they were sacred roads built by the Incas. Later, the German mathematician Maria Reiche suspected that the gigantic etchings were part of an astronomical calendar, because many of the figures and lines were perfectly aligned with the rising and setting of the sun during the solstices.

Professor Lancho described a theory held by several members of the medical community who believe that the Nazca plains may represent a map of biological evolution. If one were to rearrange the figures according to this theory, one would begin with the spiral (which represents basic unicellular life), followed by the seeds of the various plants, the great fishes, the frog (which is the first amphibian), the reptiles (which are predecessors of the birds), and then the different types of birds, from the condor, whose flight is simple, to the hummingbird, whose flight is complex. Next would come the monkey, and finally the figure called the "astronaut," which is the most baffling of all, as it is unmistakably human, with a large rounded head. According to the theory, this figure represents our next evolutionary step, when our species would leave the home planet. The rounded head, they explain, might be the helmet worn by a space traveler. Ninety percent of these figures are connected by a single line, indicating that perhaps the shaman-artists who designed the figures in the Nazca plains understood the natural sequence of evolution some fifteen hundred years ago. Could the Nazcans have foreseen our journey into the stars?

After our meeting with Professor Lancho, I explained that we could visit these figures as tourists or as persons seeking knowledge and power. Our inner attitude would determine the benefit we would obtain from our visit. We were awed by the size of figures such as a large bird, a frog, a monkey, and various animals of all types. Why and for whom were these gigantic figures built? After all, they can best be seen from an airplane. The Nazca lines and geometrical figures were closely related to water courses. Many of them also functioned as footpaths. One does not have to be in an airplane to appreciate the *lines;* most can be viewed from ground level, from the nearby foothills.[2] The medicine people of the area say that these figures are most fully appreciated during the "spirit flight," when the shaman journeys out of the body and soars through the air. But perhaps more important, the legends of the area note that each figure embodies the kind of power and knowledge represented by that animal. For example, the power of the eagle is to see life's dilemmas clearly, and to soar high above them, keeping one's eyes on more distant spiritual horizons. We found that these power animals were also represented in don Eduardo's power staffs that he places in front of his healing "mesa."

The Mesa

Native American shamans have begun to share their knowledge about healing with outsiders. A shaman uses this knowledge to heal the sick and to assist the spiritual evolution of the community. For both of these purposes, don Eduardo employs his mesa, an assemblage of power objects and staffs, many of which are thousands of years old, having been handed down from teacher to student for generations.[3]

The word *mesa* means table in Spanish, but it also means a high plateau, the place where the shaman comes to meet the spirits. Through his mesa, don Eduardo believes that he is able to work with and influence the forces of nature in order to diagnose and heal disease and help his students acquire the type of knowledge and power required to become a medicine person. The power objects are set on the ground atop a cloth that don Eduardo claims to have found in the ruins of an ancient Incan temple. On the left and right side of the mesa sit two large conch shells that the shaman explains act like antennae to receive the energy of the cosmos. The mesa is divided into three areas: the *campo ganadero* or the "field of the dark" on the left; the *campo justiciero* or "field of the light" (or justice) on the right; and the *campo medio* or the neutral field, a place of balance between the forces of light and dark. Don Eduardo claims that these forces are neither positive nor negative, but what human beings choose to do with them makes them good or evil.

The shaman's mesa included a stone shaped like a serpent, symbolizing deceit and lies. Next to it was the foreleg of a deer, used to escape from dangerous situations or to "blow" people away from certain power places, making them run like a deer in flight. Next to it was a thousand-year-old sling that the shaman used to strike blows against negative entities. Beside that was a rock shaped like a battleaxe, used for defending oneself against one's enemies. Near it was a ceramic foot, purportedly over two thousand years old, that the shaman used to track persons lost in the forest or mountains. Near the ceramic foot, a clay bat represented the forces of the night, as well as human fears. Near the bat, and forming a line going from the top to the bottom of the mesa, were a number of ceramic objects and ritual stones representing organs in the body, used by the shaman to diagnose ailments.

One of these ceramic objects was the head of a fox symbolizing an upset in the balance of life. Whenever don Eduardo sees a fox crossing his trail from left to right, he considers it an omen of bad fortune. Next to the fox head was a whistle shaped like a sleeping pelican, used to awaken feelings of sincerity and kindness in others. The middle or neutral field was dominated by an image of the sun, and below it a wooden statue of St. Cyprian, the Christian martyr, who don Eduardo claims was first a shaman and later a saint. Below St. Cyprian was a large key—the key to the doorway between the fields of light and dark. Below the key were two crystals that when struck together produced flying sparks used to ward off negative influences. On the right side, in the field of the light, were a collection of crystals and images of several Christian saints. Don Eduardo does not hesitate to combine the Christian and Indian mythologies, for he believes the Christian saints to be powerful beings of light that can be of help in diagnosing and curing illness.

Below the saints were two seashells used to drink a mixture of tobacco, alcohol, and sweet oils. The shaman uses this mixture to make an offer to Mother Earth. During the healing ceremonies don Eduardo holds in his right hand a rattle, which represents the Earth turning on its axis, and in his left a knife, a protection against the forces of the dark. On the right side of the mesa were a number of perfumes and sweet oils and a bottle of pure water to cleanse the persons that were to receive healing.

Directly before the mesa, the shaman's power staffs and swords were placed upright in the earth. On the far right was a short sabre, and next to it, a long sword representing St. Michael's sword of fire, used to cut through spiritual obstacles. The staff of the hound dog helps to find lost people and objects, while the staff of the eagle is used for calling visions and diagnosing certain kinds of disease. The staff of the seven seas, made from a swordfish bill, is used for finding lost mariners and rested to the left of the sword of St. Michael. The staff of the serpent was placed between the fields of the light and the dark and represents balance and the bringing together of the earth and heavenly energies. On the *campo ganadero,* the staff of the maiden symbolized the medicinal flowers and herbs. Next to it, an owl represented the ancient burial places and the forces of the night. And last, at the far right, was the staff of Lucifer, representing all aspects of evil, frequently the cause of illness and disease.

The shaman's mesa can be found in one form or another among many native healers in the Americas. The meaning of the symbols will vary from culture to culture, as will the specific steps in the ceremony. But all of the mesa rituals, whether in South or North America, serve as a reminder that the forces of nature and of the human psyche can be worked with when represented as symbols and objects of power.

Chapter 7

The Needle and Thread

In the evening of the fourth day of our journey we traveled to a formation known as the Needle and Thread, a figure nestled in a long narrow valley between two mountains. Like many of the other Nazca markings, the figure was over one thousand years old, and had been built by removing the uppermost layer of baked desert rock to reveal the white silica sand beneath. It was shaped like a needle, or rather, like a very thin triangle, about twenty yards wide at the base and nearly half a mile in length. A third of the way up was a large double spiral, which after seven turns zigzagged to the tip of the needle. The shaman explained that each of the turns represented one of the chakras, or energy centers of the body. Although we had visited the figure during the day, at night it was difficult to make our way through the rocks. Don Eduardo set down his mesa next to the spiral, facing east (the direction of the rising sun), where the tip of the needle pointed.

Everyone was aware that we had come to the spiral to fulfill that part of the shaman's journey that the legends refer to as "erasing our personal history," to let go of those experiences of the past that have forestalled our growth and burdened us. I could sense that my companions were both excited and afraid of the ceremony, for they knew that to "erase one's personal history" one's past had to be summoned and faced in the dark desert night. Once in a while a coyote would howl and we would look far off into the distance, wondering if this was an animal of the night, a power animal of the shaman that we would later encounter, or part of our past that haunted us.

Shortly after 10:00 P.M., don Eduardo began to call on the four winds and the spirits of the lagoons, of the forest, and of the lakes to come and take part in the healing ritual. He saluted the four corners of the world and called on the guardian spirits of the Nazca desert. After making an offering of tobacco to Mother Earth and to the heavens, he returned to his mesa, sat on a large rock, and blew sweet oil and alcohol over his power objects.

During the ceremony each person was given one of the shaman's power staffs to hold in his or her hand as we walked through the length of the spiral. One received the staff of the eagle to learn to soar high above his life's problems. Another worked with the sword of Lucifer, to learn to handle the destructive sides of her personality. Another worked with the staff of the mulatto, the half-breed horseman, to learn to control his emotions and to integrate his masculine and feminine aspects.

Between the hours of ten and twelve, the "spirits" of each of the power staffs and Christian saints represented in the shaman's mesa were called to come to take part in the healing ceremony. Both the forces of light and of darkness were summoned. Don Eduardo explained that these are two sides of the same sword and that one must remain perfectly balanced between them, dancing on the edge. The shaman then sang the songs that he claimed would call forth those experiences from our past that needed to be healed and left behind in the spiral. Don Eduardo then placed tobacco, alcohol, and herbs in one of the seashells on the mesa and offered them to the forces of nature.

Don Eduardo invited Martin, a West German physician, to be his assistant for the evening. I took my usual place at the shaman's right, the place of the "seer." We also had to make an offering to the Great Spirit and to Mother Earth by ingesting the bitter tobacco four times. The shaman explained that the mixture of herbs, tobacco, and alcohol was a powerful stimulant that awakened the visionary centers in the brain. Everyone in the group was called upon to take the mixture as don Eduardo prayed to the builders of the Nazca figures and the ancient Indian shamans. The mixture was difficult to ingest and several people coughed violently.

At midnight, everyone received a large cup of San Pedro cactus, a powerful combination of herbs that supposedly would help us step out of ordinary reality and enter the extraordinary reality of the shaman. Don Eduardo said that the San Pedro cactus would help to heal our old psychological wounds when we walked through the energy spiral.

The San Pedro mixture contained a number of psychoactive alkaloids, as do many of the ceremonial plants used by North American Indian shamans. When taking the San Pedro mixture, people typically report that their vision becomes clearer and that they are able to see the human aura and energy fields around objects. For our tribe, the San Pedro cactus created a collective vision where all of us entered into an uncommon reality, one different from the ordinary, day-to-day one. For example, nearly everyone in the group reported "seeing" one of our members go up in flames as she walked through the spiral. The shaman explained that these were painful memories from her past, particularly an "imprint" left after a long bout with cancer, that were being burned out and cleansed by the fire. Another person seemed to be followed by an older woman and a child with a dog, which almost everyone appeared to see. The shaman asked the man to identify this older woman and child. He replied that it was his mother, who had died the previous year, and that the child was himself, walking with a pet he had owned in his youth. It was curious that while don Eduardo spoke no English, and at no time volunteered information about what he "saw" when people were inside the spiral, many persons in the group reported the same perceptions as the shaman.

At three in the morning, the shaman called the woman whom we had "seen" going up in flames to come and stand before the mesa. He said that we could not take any chances with the results of her purification. We would have to create another flame, this time a physical fire, to burn out any remnants of cancer that may have afflicted her, and to prevent the recurrence of the disease. As she stood before the mesa, silhouetted against the desert sky, she said she had nearly lost her breast from cancer two years earlier, and that although she was in remission, every time she went for a checkup there were signs of a recurrence. The shaman nodded his head and said that her illness was related to an unresolved relationship with a man that continued to haunt her.

Don Eduardo made a circle of yellow cornmeal around the woman. He placed a pile of hay inside the circle and handed her St. Michael's sword of fire. Don Eduardo returned to his mesa, and taking his rattle, began a song that called for this woman's spirit and for all the causes of her illness to appear. After a few minutes of singing, he stopped, looked at her intently, and yelled "Fire!" at which point Martin and I leaped up and lit the straw beneath her. Holding the sword, she had to step across the fire four times, once in each of the four cardinal directions, and then cleanse her hands and her feet on the fire. All this time the shaman was singing a song for the healing of her spirit. Moments later, he told the woman to stomp out the fire quickly, making sure that not a single ember remained, as the fire represented the causes of her illness which had to be completely extinguished. When she finished, she was asked to take a seashell filled with tobacco and alcohol and raise it along the blade of the sword to acquire its power. She was then instructed to ingest the mixture as an offering to Mother Earth.

Two other people had to undergo the same procedure, burning up events of their past that hindered them. The shaman explained that these were experiences from this lifetime and from former lifetimes that limited their ability to fully enjoy life—physically, emotionally, mentally, and spiritually. The event might have been a traumatic death from a previous lifetime, or a psychological problem from early childhood. Don Eduardo said that understanding the causes of our problems was not nearly as important as being able to overcome and transcend them. Understanding, he claimed, was most powerful when it came after the healing. When it preceded the healing, the intellectual process often interfered and reduced it to a mere psychological experience.

The ceremony closed with the rising sun as the light of a new day began to break from the east. We all meditated silently, giving thanks to the four corners of the world, to the nature spirits, as well as to the guardians and builders of the Nazca figures, to Mother Earth and to the Great Spirit. The power objects were put away, the mesa was folded up, and, together with the staffs, were returned to the shaman's bag.

Most of us spent the long ride to Lima the following day in silence. The events of the previous evening lingered in everyone's mind. The things we had seen and felt were so out of the ordinary that it was difficult to think of the ceremony as anything other than a dream.

On our arrival in Lima that evening we gathered to share our experiences. We all spoke excitedly about what we had seen and were again surprised at the commonality of our visions. Learning to "see" was the first step to becoming a person of knowledge, I explained. At the same time that we underwent our purification in the Nazca lines, we began to develop our ability to "see," for it was our personal history that colored and tainted our vision. I encouraged the group to remain centered, as we would encounter additional tests along our path.

One such test had been experienced by Donna, a photographer from San Francisco, who said, "At one point, about four and one half hours into the ceremony, there was a force on my body that was very magnetic, and felt somewhat dangerous. I was feeling a physical and muscular sensation as if I was going to be pulled into the earth or rise up to the sky. Very frightening things were happening to me. I felt that my head was being turned against my will. I was afraid for the first time."

The shaman explained that these had been opportunities for her to develop her power. These tests were designed to throw her off center to enable her to regain her strength. He explained that the magnetic "pulling" that Donna felt toward the earth was her connection with the Great Mother. Afterward, the spirit of the San Pedro began to lift her, so that she could make a connection with the heavens and fly into other realms than those of her ordinary material existence. He explained that fear was her greatest enemy and held her back from connecting with the earth or flying to the heavens.

The shaman then demonstrated several protections against negative energies and for regaining balance. He explained that there are seven energy centers in the body, but that the one most important to protect is in the belly. This is the axis of the body and the center of one's world. To protect yourself you cross your hands over your belly, fingers extended downward. In contrast, at the time of your death, the most important center to protect is the heart. That is why the ancient Egyptian mummies were buried with their hands crossed over their hearts. The act of crossing the hands over an energy center breaks negative energy patterns or spiritual traps in which a person may be caught.

Don Eduardo was particularly pleased by the vision that one of the women in the group, a minister from San Francisco, reported. "When I was staring at the moon, it became a beautiful woman with very clear features, and I experienced love. Then it became a rose the color of a pink pearl, and the petals began to peel and it became more and more luminous; I felt close to the moon and I felt so much love. I felt as if I had love for not just the Earth, but for the universe, extending out in many concentric circles."

The shaman explained that the petals peeling from the moon were a symbol for rain. These were the tears of Grandmother Moon, being given as a gift to the Earth. During the ceremony, we had prayed for water to come down from the mountains, for there was a severe drought and the desert plains of Nazca had had no rain that year. Later that evening we heard that great floodwaters had washed down to Nazca from the mountains, carrying with them the much-needed topsoil.

Don Eduardo Calderon, Peruvian shaman and healer.

Aerial view of giant spiral in the Nazca desert plains.

Entrance to the giant spiral.
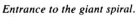

Aerial view of the hummingbird figure in the Nazca desert plains.

(PHOTO CREDIT: HANNES FLASCHBERGER)

The power objects in don Eduardo's healing "mesa."

Statue of St. Cyprian in don Eduardo's mesa. St. Cyprian is the keeper of the keys between the worlds of light and dark.

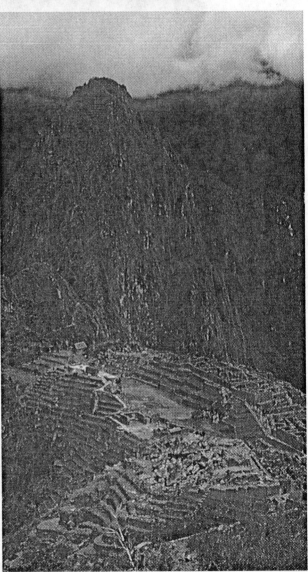

The citadel of Machu Picchu, the Inca City of Light.

Machu Picchu with Huayna Picchu in the background.

Inti Huatana, or hitching post of the Sun, the highest temple of Machu Picchu.

Temple of the Spirit Flight in Machu Picchu.

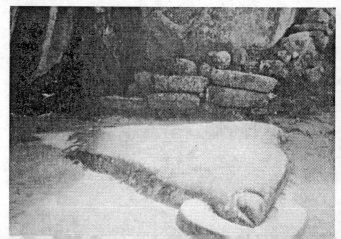

Temple of the Condor in Machu Picchu. The stone is shaped like a condor with a collar at his throat.

Entranceway to Huayna Picchu and the Temple of the Moon.

Group meditation at the altar of the Temple of the Spirit Flight, or Great Temple.

Don Eduardo's home near Drujillo.

Alberto Villoldo and don Eduardo prepare for the fire ceremony.

Energy spiral between the Temples of the Sun and Moon.

Don Eduardo holds up the sword representing the forces of the dark.

Don Eduardo takes ritual leaps to open the doorway to the spirit world.

Chapter 8

Machu Picchu

We had successfully completed the first two stages of our journey, the quest for a vision in the giant Candelabra and the cleansing and purification among the Nazca lines. In addition, the shaman said that several of us had successfully connected with our power animals during the evening ceremony at the Needle and Thread. That was a good omen, for it meant that power was pursuing us and several persons in the group were being "stalked" by their power animals. We had to remain alert, for when pursuing power we were both the hunter and the hunted. Although the power animals represented an aspect of knowledge and power, they were more than abstract symbols. The power animals are real, the shaman explained, and have an existence of their own—we had called them from their sleep and now they were following our tracks. For this reason, it was important to leave no tracks behind us. Then, when we felt the power animals near us, we would successfully stalk them.

In my earlier work with shamans I (Villoldo) found that many believed that in the course of one's life one could acquire as many as thirteen power animals. According to one of the legends, at the same instant that a human being was born, an animal was born in the forest, representing the potential wisdom and knowledge with which that person came into the world. In the book, *Man and His Symbols,* Carl Jung refers to the power animal as the "bush soul," a counterpart in nature that many "primitive" individuals believe they possess.[1] A number of the shamans I have known explain that a person frequently acquires new power animals over months and years. In their observation, persons who live in cities tend to have indolent or domesticated power animals that have grown lazy with time, and in other instances, power animals that are wild and untamed, wreaking havoc with their lives.

These animals represent an elemental energy of the forest, the winds, the waters, or fire, and become power animals only when they connect with a person. Shamans believe one can have as many as two power animals connected with each energy center in the body, except for the topmost center, which is situated at the top of the head. Here there can be only one, a transcendental power animal, usually representing sacred fire. One shaman pointed out that even in Christianity, when the Holy Spirit descended upon the twelve apostles, it was seen as a dove of fire.

When a person acquires a new power animal, that energy center becomes active, and permits an exchange of energy with nature. The shamans also point out that simply to open the energy centers without acquiring a power animal was dangerous, as one could acquire power without wisdom. Moreover, don Eduardo explained that while many of us had acquired a great deal of information during our university studies, we were not taught how to acquire "power," for information is considered powerful by the shaman only if it can be used wisely. At that point it is represented by a power animal.

For instance, one was said to acquire an eagle for a

power animal when one was able to see the future implications of one's actions or the actions of the tribe. The
shaman with an eagle "ally" would guide the tribe to the
highland caves in time to avoid the first snows or would
lead the tribal hunters to the site where a herd of caribou
would be crossing. Thus before a person was said to
have acquired a power animal, he or she had to demonstrate the ability to use knowledge powerfully for the
benefit of others.

The Temple of the Waters

Our flight landed in the city of Cuzco on the seventh day
of our journey. The morning of our arrival we rested,
and drank coca tea, a stimulating herbal drink that
helped us to acclimate to the altitude, as the city lies at
an altitude of 11,000 feet. Cuzco is a monument to the
Incas, a brilliant people who subjugated numerous tribes
in parts of what today are Peru, Ecuador, Bolivia, Co-
lombia, Chile, and Argentina. They established a system
of social security and abolished private property. Their
engineers built over 20,000 kilometers of roads through
the Andes with suspension bridges and tunnels to link
their empire. Fast relay runners were stationed every
one and a half miles; by this system, they could cover
250 kilometers a day, delivering messages in the form of
knotted strings called *kipus* or bringing fresh fish from
the coast for the emperor.[2]

That morning we had an opportunity to converse with
don Eduardo. We asked him of what importance the
mystical traditions of the shaman were for us in Europe
and North America. He replied, "It is sad that in Europe, which once had such a rich tradition of knowledge,
and where so many books are written about magic and
shamanism, there is so little practice remaining. And it is

107

unfortunate that in the seventeenth and eighteenth centuries many of the wise men and women of your cultures were tortured and burned at the stake by the church.'' He felt that although we had great literary knowledge about shamanism, and wonderful picture books and stories about North American Indian folklore, most of the practices of power and knowledge had been lost. Information without power, he said, could not be considered true knowledge. In his world view, humans followed a cycle of searching for spiritual knowledge and truth, and when they neared the point of reaching it, again collapsed into dark ages and unconsciousness. This knowledge would appear to be forgotten, only to be rediscovered again and again. Don Eduardo sees many people around the world today searching for these ancient truths.

That afternoon we traveled to the ruins of Tambo Machay, an Inca temple outside the city of Cuzco, where four underground rivers meet and break ground in a spring. We climbed behind the temple to the top of a small mountain where, after a series of breathing exercises, the shaman led us in a meditation to connect with the four important power animals of the Incas and the four streams of energy represented by the underground rivers. He asked us to find a spot on the mountain, and once we felt comfortable, to relax our bodies and begin to call on the spirits of the four power animals—the horse, the serpent, the eagle, and the jaguar. He claimed that these were the four archetypal power animals that represented the winds of the North, the South, the East, and the West.

Gradually the members of our group began to sway, adopting the posture and movements of each of the animals that the shaman invoked. When the meditation ended, several persons claimed that they had felt the presence of the animals. One commented that he saw a serpent coming from the east; another felt the spirit of the horse entering her and she began to move as if she were the animal. Others reported feeling as if they were soaring high above the mountain, riding on the wings of an eagle. As we were discussing our experiences, a sudden rainstorm broke out and we were drenched to the skin. The shaman explained that this was a cleansing rain and that we should now descend to the temple of Tambo Machay to charge each of our energy centers at the spring where the underground rivers come together.

In the temple below, three streams flow out of stones carved by the Incas more than six hundred years ago. We approached the spouts and let the water wash over our hands, and cleansed each of our seven energy centers in a counterclockwise direction. That evening we returned exhausted to our hotel, as both the altitude and the climbing had taken their toll. The shaman explained that we felt tired because the four archetypal power animals had begun to make contact with us and to realign our body energies. These animals represent a corporeal intelligence, a knowledge that is learned more readily through the body than through the mind.

In Cuzco, many of us began to have extremely vivid dreams. One woman dreamed that don Eduardo led her to the top of a high mountain, where there was a small house on a lake. Inside the house they met an old man and an old woman who started to teach her how to use medicinal plants and herbs. Don Eduardo explained that she had journeyed in her dreams to the Chimbe lagoons, and had met one of his former teachers who was instructing her in the use of healing herbs. For the shaman, dreams exist in a separate reality which an apprentice can enter to acquire the knowledge to heal and to diagnose the cause of illness.

109

The Inca City of Light

The following morning we set out with the rising sun for the ruins of Machu Picchu. Although we had only slept a few hours, we felt surprisingly refreshed, except for two of the members of our group who were suffering from *soroche,* or altitude sickness. Fortunately, Machu Picchu, at an altitude of 8,000 feet, is nearly 3,000 feet lower than the city of Cuzco. As the train descended into the Urubamba valley, our two afflicted friends began to recover.

By mid-morning we reached the base of the mountain, crossed the Urubamba river, and made our way up the winding road to the ruins at the mountaintop. Initiation rites take place even today in this ancient citadel of the Incas, which remained hidden from the eyes of outsiders until 1911 when Hiram Bingham, a young Yale University professor, was led by an Indian to the extraordinary constructions and temples at the mountaintop.

This was the first time that a group of outsiders had attempted to pass the tests and trials of shamanic initiation, and don Eduardo explained that none of his apprentices could enter Machu Picchu before undergoing a ritual death. This was especially true of the "power spots"—certain parts of the ruins that we should not enter because our opening to the spirit world had made us vulnerable. The shaman explained that there were spirit guardians protecting these ancient ruins and that we must ask their permission to enter, particularly in Machu Picchu, the most powerful center of all. If they did not accept us, we would have to take the next train back to Cuzco. Don Eduardo explained that we must spend the night in meditation in the outskirts of the ruins, calling on the spirit guardians of the citadel. As it turned out, we were to undergo not only spiritual tests, but physical ones as well.

110

After hiking for nearly two miles over a narrow mountain path, we arrived at the Doorway of the Sun which had a commanding view of the citadel as well as of the Urubamba River, which winds around it like a protective serpent. A few stone walls, the remains of an ancient gatekeeper's house, were all that was left of the Doorway of the Sun. We gathered firewood as soon as we arrived, and built a fire under the last rays of the setting sun. Don Eduardo brought out his rattle and knife and began to sing, calling on the spirits of the four winds and on the guardians of Machu Picchu. He invited their tests, telling them that we had come in good will ready to accept our death, to learn the spirit flight, and to pay our respects at the Inti Huatana, the stone where the Incas worshipped the sun.

After over an hour of songs of meditation, someone pointed to a clump of bushes twenty feet away, on the edge of the jungle. We perceived an eerie light shaped like a person, with a large, rounded head. The apparition sent shivers through everyone in the group. The shaman said that we should remain centered, that this was sent by one of the guardians to test us before we would be allowed to enter the citadel. The figure hovered in the bushes, sometimes coming nearer, and then receding into the jungle. Don Eduardo warned us not to leave the medicine circle, but Clara felt nauseous and began to wander about the ruins. Two members of the group went out in search of her, and found Clara completely disoriented, feeling weak, and lacking the willpower to continue with the healing ceremony. She was brought back to the circle, and don Eduardo explained that this was an example of the type of test we would encounter.

Close to midnight, the shaman said that those of us who preferred could remain by the fire, meditating on the embers, but that he would advise sleep, as we had a long day ahead of us tomorrow. If at any time during the night we experienced fear, we should return to the calming circle of the fire. He explained that the luminous apparition was "an elemental being," created by the old shamans of Machu Picchu to test those who wanted to enter the citadel. If one was not prepared psychologically and spiritually, one could lose one's way in the jungle, running the danger of falling off the mountain.

We were surprised by the shaman's warnings because, with the exception of Clara, everyone felt a sense of peace and tranquility in the clear, star-filled night. Except for the brief appearance of the "being" in the bushes, we felt welcomed by the ruins. Yet no sooner had we settled into our sleeping places on the ground than we heard a scream. Michael, an Austrian engineer, had decided to take a short walk before retiring and had stumbled upon an ancient Inca stairway covered by the underbrush. Indeed, he had fallen down the stairs. The first person to reach him was Clara, who also lost her footing and fell down a steep well. Fortunately, the well was overgrown with vines and she was able to cling to the edge until help arrived. Clara suffered only a few scratches and a bruised pride. Michael, on the other hand, had sprained his ankle and was barely able to walk. Don Eduardo explained that these were our tests, that one cannot enter a place of power irresponsibly. Chastised, we returned to our sleeping places, only to be awakened twenty minutes later by an icy thunder shower.

Initiation by Death

Although none of us had slept for more than an hour the entire night, the following morning we were full of anticipation. I was aware that the most powerful results occurred from the preparation for the death ceremony to take place later in the day, when one looks at the loose ends and the unfinished relationships from the past that often litter our lives. It is not that we are normally unaware of these events of our past, but rather that our awareness does not lead us to do anything about them. The preparation consisted of motivating us to clean up the decades of debris accumulated in our lives.

In the early morning hours, the ritual itself was performed atop a canoe-shaped stone pointing directly to the West. A ring was carved in the front of the stone so that the spirits of the dead could pull the canoe to the sunset. One by one, each of us lay on top of the stone. The shaman touched the seven energy centers of each participant and asked that his or her spirit be taken to the West to meet its death. "May the winds of the South take the canoe to the regions of silence and death," he said, "and then back to life." The legends say that a person's spirit returns from the East where the sun rises and from where new life emerges. The initiates, the legends continue, are born again in spirit as "Incas," as Children of the Sun.

Although the ritual lasted only three to four minutes per person, time seemed to disappear. Several people reported feeling as if they had flown out of their bodies, speeding down a dark tunnel. Others reported a wrenching sensation each time the shaman passed his hands over one of their energy centers. When my turn came, I felt as though I were sinking deeply into the earth, losing consciousness of my body yet still hearing the group chanting in the background. I felt as if I had been swallowed by the earth, and suddenly had the unsettling thought that this must be what it felt like to be in a coffin. At that moment I resolved that when I died, my body would be cremated. I relished the thought of being consumed by fire, freed from any physical encumbrance. Later don Eduardo explained that learning to die was one of the most important lessons for a shaman's apprentice. The ceremony ended when the shaman thanked the spirit masters of Machu Picchu, striking a pair of cymbals to close the doorway to the spirit world.

Next, our group proceeded through the main entrance into Machu Picchu, the Incan City of Light. We followed the shaman to an open area where the Great Temple once stood. All that remained of the structure were three massive walls and a stone bed that occupied the southwest corner of the temple. I explained that the bed was used for the spirit flight, or out-of-body experience, through which the shaman is able to journey into the lower worlds to find the causes of disease, and into the upper worlds to determine the outcome of events, and even to influence the course of a person's destiny. The shaman claims that the spirit flight, or learning to leave the physical body, will be most important when we die; without this knowledge the spirit can be confused for years, lost between this world and the next.

The object of the exercise was to visit, during the spirit flight, the Temple of the Moon atop Huayna Picchu, an adjoining peak that towers one thousand feet above Machu Picchu. During the spirit flight meditation, the shaman asked us to travel to the top of Huayna Picchu and to "see" the energy symbols that are inscribed on the Moon Temple. He explained that these symbols, made up of circles within triangles, were once etched on the portals of the temple, but that the temple had long since been destroyed. Yet, he claimed, these symbols remained as "energy forms" that could be seen during the spirit flight.

At the close of the meditation several members of our group reported seeing a cross enclosed within a golden circle, as well as a series of concentric golden triangles rotating in space. Don Eduardo said these were two of the sacred symbols of the temple, but that we had failed to see the most important one, a sun surrounded by two half moons in the shape of a cat, which depicts the marriage of the Sun and Moon, the integration of masculine and feminine aspects.

We felt dwarfed in the Andes, but nowhere so much as in the awesome vastness surrounding Machu Picchu. To one side a gorge drops for two thousand feet, and on another side Huayna Picchu climbs steeply, then tapers like the body and tail of a crouching lion, nearly enclosed by the roaring Urubamba River.

I had had a memorable experience with don Eduardo on a visit to Machu Picchu three years earlier. I always believed in the eternity of the spirit, although I never believed that one could experience this before death. The first time I lay on the stone of the spirit flight and felt the shaman place his hand on my forehead, I felt a great peace and relaxation. Yet nothing unusual occurred. I did not soar like an eagle, nor did I find the peak of Huayna Picchu. After what appeared to be ten minutes, don Eduardo said, "Okay, come up." I sat up from the stone and walked away to join my companions in the circle. To my surprise, everyone was looking intently at the stone bed. I turned around and saw my physical body—and a smiling don Eduardo signaling for me to come back and lie again on the stone so as to reconnect with my physical self.

Inti Huatana

On a small hill twenty yards from the Great Temple is the Inti Huatana, the fabled "hitching post of the sun." Each year, at the winter solstice, the Incas staged a ceremony to "tie the sun," lest it swing even farther north in its daily arc and be lost forever. It is said that when Hiram Bingham reached Machu Picchu in 1911, he reported seeing an additional stone on top of the Inti Huatana. Don Eduardo believes that this was a crystal used

115

to communicate with shamans in distant parts of the planet and in other dimensions of time and space. The Inti Huatana is said to be the place where the Earth and the Sun meet. It is important to be at the stone as the first rays of the rising sun break over the mountaintops and strike the rock. The shamanic legends say that when one touches one's forehead to the stone, the Inti Huatana opens one's vision into the spirit world.

Although it had been light for nearly two hours, the sun was only now breaking over the mountaintops and casting its first rays on the Sun Temple. We formed a circle around the Inti Huatana and, one at a time, knelt before the stone, touching our foreheads to the altar itself. Several members of our group felt a sensation of warmth on their foreheads, even though the mountain air was brisk and the stone felt cool to the touch. Others reported seeing a light go on inside their heads like a bursting sun. Don Eduardo dismissed these reports, claiming that the real effect of the ceremony would not be felt for weeks as each of us learned the shaman's way to "see" and to recognize that we were all children of the Sun, living beings of light.

When we asked don Eduardo what he meant by learning to "see," he replied that a shaman was not able to "see" with his or her inner vision until his or her feminine side was awakened. Our masculine, rational side, he claimed, allowed us to see only the surface of things. We would not awaken the feminine side of ourselves until later that afternoon at the Pachamama stone.

At three in the afternoon we gathered at the Pachamama, a stone over twenty feet long and ten feet high that represents Mother Earth. This was the final stage of a twenty-four-hour-long ceremony in the citadel of Machu Picchu. Don Eduardo explained that in the Inti Huatana we connected with the energies of the sun and awakened the masculine side of ourselves. At the stone of the Pachamama we would awaken the feminine side of ourselves and connect with Mother Earth. The stone represents fertility, not only of the earth and of women, but also of the mind.

This time we approached the stone in pairs, one man and one woman, each carrying an offering of fruits or flowers which we placed before the stone of the Mother Earth. We then pressed our backs against the stone and prayed we would be welcomed by the Great Mother, before we returned to her at our deaths. In our prayer, we asked that she teach us about the seasons, about the ripening of the fruits, about fertility, about how all blossoms must fall back to earth to endure long winters and flower again in the spring. As we finished our prayer, the shaman blessed us, entreating the Earth to become our teacher and asking that we help others learn to live in balance with the Earth.

The shaman explained that in Huayna Picchu, the mountain behind the Pachamama, was the Temple of the Moon, with labyrinths and tunnels whose secret entrances were sealed from the eyes of the uninitiated but were clearly marked to the eyes of the shaman. The legends say there is an old medicine woman who lives within the mountain, to whom the shamans come for their highest initiations, those that lead into the Nagual, or the feminine component of reality. The caverns inside the mountain are said to be used as often today as they were during the time of the Incas, for shamanism is a tradition of knowledge that is not bound to a time or culture.

We finished the ritual at the Pachamama at four o'clock, barely in time to catch our train. Everyone slept, for we were physically exhausted from engaging in almost constant activity for nearly forty hours. Yet perhaps that same physical exhaustion was allowing us to step into the extraordinary reality of the shaman by helping us break down cultural barriers that defined the limits of our perception.

It was difficult for us to imagine what don Eduardo meant by the "feminine." The French anthropologist Claude Lévi-Strauss claimed that the thinking of the primitive and that of the modern person were equally valid but fundamentally different.[3] Primitive people believed that you could not understand anything until you understood everything. In other words, you could not understand how a blade of grass grew if you did not understand the workings of the universe. In contrast, modern people believe that you cannot understand the cosmos until you understand the blade of grass, down to its atomic structure. This might be the best way to compare "feminine" thinking with the "masculine" approach of the Western world. Shamanism and modern science seem to approach knowledge from opposite ends of the spectrum, yet both provide us with a coherent image of reality.

Chapter 9

Black Magic

The following day we boarded our flight to the northern Peruvian desert, only a few miles from the coast, to visit Don Eduardo's home, a rustic adobe house that he himself had built next to the ocean.

The shaman lives with his wife and six of his fourteen children in a village twenty miles south of the city of Trujillo. I had not seen his wife Maria and the children in nearly a year, and they ran out to greet us when we arrived. The house had not changed since my last visit, except for the thatched roofs that showed signs of wear and tear from the recent rainstorms. Directly across from their home Maria and the children had opened a small restaurant where a single course of fried fish was prepared in a variety of ways, with potatoes, with bananas, and with rice and sea urchin or manta ray, all of which they had prepared for our arrival. Don Eduardo suggested that we perform the "*cui* cleansings" on the members of our group before lunch.

The guinea pig, or *cui,* is used by shamans throughout Peru to diagnose disease. The animal is rubbed over the seven energy centers of a person's body. The guinea pig is thought to be like a primitive X-ray, as the animal's organs are said to reveal any signs of organic disease that may afflict the patient.

But most important, the *cui* is used to diagnose sorcery. If the person is suffering from black magic the guinea pig's spine will snap and the animal will die as it is rubbed over the patient's body. Don Eduardo explained that "from ancient times, on the coast as well as the mountains, shamans have used the guinea pig for diagnosis. The animal is supersensitive, and absorbs any negativity or illness of the energy centers, as well as any nervous disorders."

The guinea pig must be skinned alive, and its organs examined while its heart is still beating. Don Eduardo correctly diagnosed the physical ailments that several members of our group suffered from, explaining that while many of the symptoms of disease had disappeared, in many cases the underlying cause of the illness was still present and showed up on the *cui*. But what surprised us the most was that several of the guinea pigs appeared with a broken spine. This agreed with my observation that the most deadly kind of black magic is that which we unconsciously perpetrate against ourselves. In Western medicine, we refer to these as psychosomatic disorders and stress-related illnesses, which may even include some types of cancers.

That evening we scheduled a fire ritual for those who had been diagnosed as suffering from sorcery. We spent the remainder of the day meditating to discover which incidents in our lives had predisposed us to perform "black magic" on ourselves. We also contemplated the behavior and habit patterns that obstructed our happiness and success. Those whose guinea pigs had shown no sign of illness or sorcery were encouraged to meditate on what aspects of their lives were ready to be left behind, and which they wanted to place into the fire.

After a sumptuous meal of fried fish, we gathered in a

circle outside don Eduardo's home. After two weeks of difficult travel, the members of our group felt exhausted. Our psyches had been challenged with new information and experiences that stretched the limits of our consciousness. In addition, the night-long healing ceremonies had begun to strip away our defenses, and don Eduardo believed that our group was now at a point where we could approach the holy fire that would burn away our past. The danger, he explained, was to return to our comfortable habits once we returned to our homes, for this would obviate any shamanic knowledge we had acquired. This would be the greatest hurdle we would have to overcome. The shaman invited us to share those parts of our past we wished to place into the fire.

Donna, the photographer from San Francisco, commented that during her life she had been feeling everyone else's pain and coming to their aid, but that she had never taken care of herself. "I know I want to be a people helper," she said, "and I want to learn to help the land. My next step is to learn to care for myself." Donna went on to explain that by being so engaged with the lives of others, she avoided having to think about her own needs.

Eva, the Austrian architect, said, "Last night, for the first time in ten years, I danced. It was a very sad event that led me to stop dancing. Yesterday the time had obviously come for me to dance again." She was referring to a surprise birthday party we had held the previous evening, where, together with don Eduardo's children, we had danced to the sound of an old radiola. Eva explained that since her separation from her husband she had been unwilling to open herself to a new and lasting relationship. Both Donna and Eva had identified problems that psychotherapists would consider psychological. However, don Eduardo pointed out that as shaman's apprentices we had to learn to face these issues and not postpone dealing with them, for death could strike us at any moment, and the shaman was always prepared to die.

Other group members related problems which were of a more existential or spiritual nature. Rainer, a psychologist from West Germany, claimed that he felt as if he were in the middle of a dark night of the soul. He said, "I feel I'm part of a process of complete dissolution where I know less and less every day. I no longer have any idea of what I want and why I came here."

Rainer commented that those matters which used to have value in his life no longer seemed meaningful. He hoped to discover a new vision for his life, and the strength to make the necessary changes, such as moving to the southern part of the country where he felt more at home but where he did not have the security of work or friends.

For the last year, Clara, the Spanish management consultant, had experienced many strange occurrences, such as objects that would mysteriously disappear, or hearing strange noises throughout the house. Don Eduardo said that these were signs of her developing psychic abilities and that she had to learn to control her power, otherwise this power would express itself in a destructive and uncontrollable manner. Clara observed, "In the last three years of my life, I have moved through very deep personal problems but I did not know that it was going to be so horrible. I was completely in darkness. Many of the experiences we have had here, I have seen in my dreams. I felt completely unbalanced. Yet when I arrived here, my contact with nature helped a lot. And tonight, for the first time in these three years, I think I feel some balance. I see that when asking for light, I first have to ask for healing."

Each of us spent the remainder of the afternoon searching for a piece of driftwood that we had to carve as a representation of the parts of our past that we wanted to change. Don Eduardo told me that the broken spine in my guinea pig resulted from the emotional pain surrounding my recent divorce. He said that it was not a matter of who had been right or wrong. Rather, it was a matter of carrying on with life and helping my ex-wife as much as possible to do the same. It was true that the bitterness and pain I carried in my heart were turning everything in my life sour. The path of the shaman, don Eduardo explained, is to leave no loose ends in his or her life, and to be prepared for death at every instant.

As I walked on the beach picking up and discarding pieces of driftwood that were too long, too short, or not the right shape, I felt it was possible that marriages, like people, had a natural life span. The fact that my relationship had ended did not mean that it was a failure, in the same way that when we died it did not mean that our lives had been fruitless. After walking for nearly three hours, I came upon a piece of wood with a knot in the middle. The center of the knot was gone, leaving a hole that made the piece of wood seem like a natural looking glass. With my pocket knife, I rounded the rough edges of the hole and carved a wavy design onto the stem to represent the wind. Then, without knowing why, I etched the figure of a bird in flight. When I placed the stick in the fire later that evening, I felt as if a knot in my heart had been loosened and I had been set free again.

The Holy Fire

Later that evening, we gathered in a small plot of land where don Eduardo grows medicinal plants. The shaman sat in the center by a small pile of wood, holding a sword in one hand and a rattle in the other. After calling the spirit of the four winds and making an offering to Mother Earth, he asked me to light the fire. The fire would not start, but don Eduardo did not notice, as he was shaking his rattle and singing with his eyes closed. The group also chanted, calling the spirits of the waters that ran deep beneath the earth to come and purify us. After several attempts, the fire finally sparked and began to send up clouds of smoke.

Don Eduardo explained that the fire did not start because we had not approached it with enough respect or been sincere about the offering that we prepared. The purpose of the fire was to leave behind our problems and illness, and also to offer the best of ourselves to the Great Spirit. The shaman blew sweet oil and perfume into the fire and made an offering to the four winds with a red liquid that represented our blood returning to Mother Earth.

After we had chanted for nearly two hours, the fire seemed to change color and the flames acquired a bluish hue. This was a sign that the fire had become friendly and that we could now come and place our offerings in the flames. One by one, we approached the fire. As our offering burned, we placed our hands in the flames, bringing the fire to our forehead, to our hearts, and to our bellies. The shamanic traditions state that our hands were protected from injury because the inner fire within each one of us had come to life. It had become a holy fire, don Eduardo explained, that could carry our offerings to the Great Spirit.

The New Shamans

When we asked don Eduardo why he had agreed to work with our group, he replied that it was important to bring the ancient shamanic knowledge into the world again. "When the Europeans arrived in America," he said, "many of the native American shamans were forced to withdraw from the public eye, so they retreated from the villages into the mountains and jungles. Yet our prophecies speak about the return of the buffalo, and the time when the white man will set foot on the Grandmother Moon. This is the time to make these teachings public again." Don Eduardo's teachers had said that when a person comes with open hands and a good heart, asking to be taught, the teacher has an obligation to share his knowledge.

Don Eduardo's teachers live in the mountain lagoons of northern Peru, in an area that can be reached only after several days of travel by horseback and on foot. This location kept their predecessors safe from the long arm of the Inquisition and today protects them from prosecution by the Peruvian medical establishment. Don Eduardo himself has had numerous clashes with local authorities who have accused him of practicing medicine without a license. Only in the last few years has this attitude changed, and he has been approached by medical students to intern with him to understand Native American concepts of illness and healing. Over 80 percent of the Peruvian population are Indians, most of whom still adhere to the traditional beliefs but whose native medicine is ill-equipped to deal with the illnesses of civilization. Don Eduardo recognizes the importance of a partnership with Western medicine, and believes that through cooperation, native and allopathic healers can help resolve many of humanity's ills. This was one of the principal reasons he had agreed to work with our group. Some writers have raised legitimate concerns regarding "guided tours" to visit sacred power spots.[1] In our case, however, we were invited by don Eduardo and our trip took on the nature of an initiatory journey, not a sightseeing expedition.

Chapter 10

Between Heaven and Earth

The following day the shaman informed us that I and several others whose guinea pig had had a broken spine would have to undergo a treatment for "black magic" that evening.

At 10:00 P.M. we arrived on the outside walls of the Temple of the Dragon, a monumental structure protected by a thick adobe wall. Don Eduardo made an owl-like hoot and a few moments later a wiry old man appeared, unlocked the gate, and led us to the inner temple. The cloister was a large rectangle, surrounded by twelve meditation chambers that extended from three of its sides. The only way to enter these chambers was by lowering ourselves, one at a time, with the aid of a thick rope, down the fifteen-foot drop.

At some earlier time it must have been possible to enter these rooms directly from the body of the main temple, but in the centuries following the Spanish conquest, after the temple had been abandoned and fallen into disrepair, these entrances had either caved in or been sealed by the priests to prevent access to the inner and more sacred chambers. Don Eduardo explained that there were still secret entrances to the inner temple, tun-

126

nels that were used by master shamans for their rituals inside the cloister.

We sat inside the outermost meditation chamber, and don Eduardo asked me to step into the center and face him. The shaman's assistants then made a circle around me with yellow corn and placed a bundle of straw at my feet. At don Eduardo's signal, they set the straw on fire. The shaman instructed me to walk across the flames, following an intricate pattern of steps, all the while holding a sword in fighting position in my right hand.

Don Eduardo then instructed me to place first my hands and then my feet briefly into the flames to purify them. Afterward, he "read" each of us who had undergone the purification by fire. The shaman said he saw a rope tightly wound around my stomach, incapacitating me. I mentioned that in the last few weeks I had been suffering from chronic stomach problems, and frequently had had to take antacids and digestive enzymes.

The shaman went on to explain that my problem was not with my digestion, but with the power center located at my solar plexus. A tall, dark-haired woman was robbing my power, he said, weakening me emotionally in a way that affected my work and every other aspect of my life, even my digestion. Indeed, I had been having difficulties with a woman friend who fit the shaman's description, yet I had not made much of the situation, especially as she was in the United States and I was in South America. Don Eduardo explained that the fire had burned the "ropes" tying me to her and that I should expect this relationship to change on my return to the United States.

Although my stomach problems did not subside, over the next few days I felt an increased sense of energy and stamina. And on my return to the United States, I was pleased to discover that the woman don Eduardo saw as doing "black magic" on me had overcome her bitterness and was interested in reestablishing our friendship.

San Pedro

For our first healing ritual on the Nazca plains don Eduardo had prepared a strong mixture of San Pedro cactus that contained herbs for purifying the blood, cleansing the bowels, and renewing the body in general. This time the San Pedro mixture contained visionary plants, the sacred herbs that don Eduardo uses to open up the inner vision. The shaman warned us that it was important to remain focused so as to avoid being trapped by hallucinations—images that could become distortions of reality. Instead, we were to keep our eyes open, concentrating on his power staffs directly in front of his mesa.

Every so often, I noticed that several persons were dozing off, overcome by fatigue and the seductive effect of the San Pedro mixture. Once or twice I stood up to rouse one of these persons, but the shaman motioned me to sit down. Instead he directed his look toward the sleeping individual and began to whistle the song of that person's power animal. Within an instant, the person would bolt upright, open his or her eyes wide, and look around with surprise. In the course of the evening, a number of our companions reported seeing shapes in the form of their power animals in the center of our circle. Often, these were misty figures of a bird, a fox, or a bear that would approach one or another person in the group.

It was difficult to keep our eyes open and focused on the shaman's power staffs. Even if we had not been physically exhausted, the San Pedro mixture took us into an altered state of consciousness in which our everyday awareness began to fade. Yet if we did not remain awake the shaman would consider us weak-willed and unlikely candidates for shamanic initiation. One of the people in the group reported, "The only way I could remain alert was by sitting on a pointed rock that dug into my skin. But even the pain was not enough at times and I would catch myself dozing off. In those moments I would feel myself like a great white bird with wings outstretched, flying over the entire world. Sometimes I would be flying over the desert and notice the shaman with his rattle, the mesa, the power objects, and my companions. I would then open my eyes and see the same scene, but from the perspective of the ground. I would then catch myself and realize that this was one of the traps of which don Eduardo had spoken. These experiences, he said, were only valid when done with full awareness. Although I was experiencing a vision, it was a vision with little power, for it was confined to the realm of fantasy." The objective, the shaman explained, was to be fully conscious during our visions.

From my past experiences with don Eduardo, I knew that when he whistled his power songs, the forces of nature personified as the "Aukis," the "Apos," the "Huamanes," and the "Pacarinas" would appear. These were the spirits of the lakes, the forests, and the lagoons. If one had the power of shamanic vision, one would be able to see these spirits in the center of and around the medicine circle. That night, a number of persons claimed to have seen them and to have glimpsed the power animals of the group.

The following day we visited the ruins of Chan Chan, a city built during the height of the Mochica culture. The Mochicas were producing textiles and ceramics over two thousand years before the rise of the Incas. Don Eduardo had worked for fifteen years excavating and restoring the ruins. In a courtyard bounded by high adobe walls we shared the experiences of the previous evening. Rainer, the German psychologist, recalled that he had begun fall-

129

ing asleep long before he took the San Pedro. "At the moment I sat down on my spot," he said, "I had the feeling that the spot itself was putting me to sleep."

Don Eduardo explained, "Sometimes we feel disconnected, and then we get hold of ourselves, and come back. This is another of the tests of the medicine man, to resist the temptation of losing consciousness when one leaves the material world and enters the world of the spirit." Even don Eduardo was affected by this problem, explaining that at times he would feel himself dozing off, seduced into sleep by the power of the desert spirits.

The shaman's apprentice must fight to remain conscious; only when he or she succeeds is it possible to attain the knowledge and wisdom that for centuries novices have sought to acquire. Don Eduardo explained that one does not become a person of knowledge instantly. "There are people," he said, "who think that the path of shamanism is not interesting enough or is too difficult, for they attain no great achievements at the start." The shaman explained that we each learn at our own pace and we must be patient and persevere even if we do not meet with success in our first or second attempt. "There are people who are born awake," don Eduardo said, "and people who wake up in the morning. Some of us wake up at midday, and some of us don't wake up at all in the course of our lives."

The visionary plants that we had ingested the previous evening were to help us suspend ordinary reality and step out of our culture-bound thinking patterns. Shamans in South America typically believe that one is not able to enter the world of the spirit until one can suppress the "chatter" that continually goes on inside the brain. This "inner-brain chatter," whether it be a dialogue or a song rambling through our minds, preserves through words and music the reality that we learned in our homes and schools and that defines the limits of human capabilities.

Shamans believe that we live as prisoners of a cultural trance, blindly inhabiting a small corner of the universe of possibilities. The San Pedro cactus opens the doorway to a new reality where nothing is assumed to be true or false until it is tested.

This is a point of view that closely resembles the model of reality held by the physics of quantum mechanics. Quantum Theory can be interpreted to state that our material world is created again and again before our eyes each instant we perceive it. Thus the nature of reality is in the eyes of the beholder, in the act of beholding itself. The shaman takes this one step further, believing that if you can change your perception of reality, you can actually influence events in the material world. Thus if one can change one's perception of illness, one can influence and accelerate the ordinary course of healing. If one can change one's perception of a neighboring tribe, one can bring about peace with that tribe. Thus reality, from the point of view of the shaman, emerges from an individual's or society's expectations.

There is an ancient story from Persia that illustrates this point. Two travelers who were headed in opposite directions met by the roadside. The first traveler asked what kind of people he would find in the town toward which he was headed. In response, the second traveler inquired how he had found the city that he had just left. The first replied, "They were thieves and charlatans. I did not meet a single honest person among them. The streets were filthy and the people lived like animals among the garbage." The traveler replied, "Then that is exactly what you will find in the next city!"

The Power Staffs

In our travels we had undergone a ritual of purification at the giant markings of Nazca and, before that, a symbolic death in the ruins of Machu Picchu, where we had connected with the "masculine" forces of the Sun Temple. The time had come to encounter "feminine" forces in the Temple of the Moon.

After visiting Chan-Chan, we drove to the temple and prepared the site for our evening ritual. The temple was built by the Mochicas thousands of years ago and is held to be the oldest adobe structure in the Americas. Nearly three hundred feet long and more than fifty feet high, the once mighty structure is now almost completely covered by the desert sand, and there are gaping holes in its side where robbers have attempted to loot its treasures.

The previous night we had climbed to the top of a mountain directly behind the Temple of the Moon. It was a difficult and dangerous ascent, as the lower half of the mountain was sandy and the upper half was a kind of shale that crumbled under our steps. The climb tested our endurance and determination, and we had to rely on what the shaman called our "inner vision" to guide us through the tortuous and often slippery trail at night.

The members of our group were past the point of exhaustion; yet although we had barely slept, there was a life force and energy that all of us experienced. Although this was the first time that don Eduardo had taken a group of non-Indians through the journey of shamanic initiation, he was not making the journey easy for us. On the contrary, he was testing the limits of our endurance and determination. If we were going to fail in our shamanic quest he wanted us to fail now, before we harmed anyone else or ourselves.

The Temple of the Moon had been a sacred place for shamans of the Mochica for over 2,500 years. Here apprentices would come to learn the healing arts, as well as to meet the spirit of the ancient shaman master, a woman whom the traditions say is buried inside the temple. The medicine men and women of the area believe that the wisdom of this old shaman continues to radiate to all those who come to this temple with the proper attitude.

Each of us went to meditate alone in the temple. Don Eduardo had loaned each individual one of his power staffs which represented an aspect of shamanic knowledge that he or she needed to acquire. The staff of the owl represented the ancient burial places and nocturnal powers. The staff of the eagle, with the head and feet of an eagle tied to it, represented flight and vision. Each of the thirteen staffs represented knowledge about the natural world. The staff was to help us tap the energy of the Temple of the Moon, and to serve as a protection in case the energy was too great and threatened to affect us adversely.

For most of us the experiences in the Temple of the Moon were quite intense. Martin, the German physician, reported that he could remember nothing of the evening, yet he knew that he did not fall asleep, for throughout the next day images and recollections of the previous night would come into his mind. Deborah, a California solar energy specialist, reported that she was fighting her state of exhaustion so much that she could not do anything else. "The whole thing just went by," she said, "because I was simply preoccupied with staying on my feet."

It appears that the knowledge of the Nagual—the "overworld" or "feminine" component of reality—is one that does not lend itself readily to logical or verbal expression. The medicine men and women themselves refer to it as a "wisdom that can only be experienced through song or art, not in words." Don Eduardo explained that this "wisdom" would have a continuing effect on us over the following weeks and months. The shaman explained that during our dreams we could enter this "overworld," the realm of the spirit. Yet as we did not know how to make proper use of our dreams, our journeys were still superficial in nature.

In the Temple of the Moon, many of us had stepped into the "overworld," yet lost consciousness in the process. That is why the meditations in this temple are always done on one's feet. Yet, although we kept moving all night, very few of us had any recollection of what had transpired; our memories were only of basic physical and emotional sensations.

Don Eduardo believes that in the journey to the "overworld" we acquire information about the evolution of the spirit and the destiny of our species. With this knowledge, the shaman becomes an evolutionary agent, learning the techniques for preserving and unfolding an evolutionary plan which the trees, the stars, and we humans obey.

It requires years to master the journey to the "overworld." Don Eduardo later explained that during the evening we had faced a number of tests. He had watched us closely; depending on how each of us responded to the energies of the Temple of the Moon, he determined whom he would initiate as novice shamans the following day. He confided to me that the energy fields of those persons who had no recollection of the events of the evening had almost disappeared, as their energy bodies withdrew to the familiar solace of the physical self. On the other hand, those who had remained alert and wakeful during the night were filled with a radiant energy that enlarged their bodies' energy field.

That afternoon we built a stone spiral on the desert floor between the temples of the Sun and Moon. The previous evening we had had our first glimpse into the "overworld." It had been a shock to step outside of our ordinary reality, and now we had to regain our sense of balance by walking into the medicine spiral. (The spiral is a form characterizing many objects in the universe, from the Milky Way to the DNA molecule.) In the medicine spiral, we symbolically journeyed to the center of the Earth.

The spiral was situated between the temples of the Sun and the Moon, perfectly balanced in the same way that a human being should be—between masculine and feminine, and between Heaven and Earth. After two hours of chanting in the desert sun we disassembled the spiral, scattering the rocks in the desert, as don Eduardo said we could not leave behind any trace of our visit.

Chapter 11

Initiation

In the last few weeks our group had been following the steps and undergoing the trials for becoming a person of knowledge. Those who were initiated would be invited to become caretakers of the Earth.

Don Eduardo invited us to go to a spring-fed lagoon in the desert a few hours south of Trujillo, a power spot held sacred by the shamans of the area. For centuries shamans had brought their students to this lagoon for their initiations, but this was the first time that a group of North Americans and Europeans had visited it. After a long drive through desert marshes, we reached a wide and shallow lake. It was eleven o'clock and our ceremony had to begin sharply at noon. We hiked to a spot directly facing the east, don Eduardo thrust a large sword in the sand, and we all lined up in a half-moon behind him on the water's edge. We had brought with us a variety of personal objects and several silver coins wrapped in cloth to throw into the lagoon, to symbolically anchor our spirits to that spot. At twelve sharp, with the sun high overhead, don Eduardo began to whistle and shake his rattle, calling on the spirits of the four winds and making an offering of corn to the four directions. He called on the Aukis, Apus, Huamanes, and

Pacarinas (the spirits of the lakes, the lagoons, and the forests), for the shamans believe that the spirit of the Earth herself flows into these desert lagoons. He called on his teachers and recited a prayer to the masters that had been initiated over the centuries at this lagoon.

Earlier that day the shaman had explained that there were dangers involved in the initiation. It was possible for the apprentice to suffer "loss of soul," during which psychological problems and psychosomatic disturbances could become manifest. To ensure our safety, don Eduardo took several mouthfuls of cananga, a red herbal essence that represented human blood. He blew it into the lagoon while praying, "With the juice of the good cananga, I go striking blows against my enemies, against all forces of the dark, and against all negativity." Smoking wild jungle tobacco, he called on the waters to open, as the lagoons were doorways to the spirit world. For the remainder of the hour, don Eduardo called on the spirits of the trees, plants, and all the power animals to be present during the initiation.

There was a great feeling of expectation in our group, for nobody knew whom the shaman would initiate. In the dozen or so years that I had known don Eduardo, he had initiated fewer than ten of his students and never had he indicated that he felt I was ready for this step. To my surprise, he turned to me and said that I would be first. I stepped up to the shaman and received a lime, which I took with me into the lagoon. I headed for the spot where we earlier had set three staffs to mark the place where our physical world ended and the "overworld" began. I bit into the lime and blew its juice three times as an offering to the waters. I then threw my offering, which I had carefully wrapped and prepared that morning, into the center of the lagoon. I heard don Eduardo's chants floating across the water as he prayed that my spirit be guarded and anchored to this ancient power center. The shaman's song seemed to flow gently over the water and reverberate through the lagoon, as if a dozen voices were singing. I looked to the spot where my offering had landed and saw the reflection of the noonday sun captured in the center of the lake.

I then heard don Eduardo whistle, warning me not to lose my concentration. I dropped into the water and washed, cleansing myself of the past, for many traditions state that to be born again as a shaman one must set aside one's personal history. As I walked back to don Eduardo, I noticed he was holding his *seguro,* a bottle given to him by his teacher and filled with herbs from the high mountain lagoons. These herbs are mixed with lime juice, alcohol, and sweet oils, and represent don Eduardo's connection with his spiritual body.

Suddenly, don Eduardo blew a mouthful of liquid from his *seguro* at me, symbolically breathing new life into my spirit. He then crossed my body with his sword in the four directions to cut the connections with the person I used to be. He spun me so that I rolled on the earth, symbolically born again—this time not of a woman, but of the Great Earth Mother herself.

Less than one third of the members of our group were initiated that day. Yet even those not initiated were invited to make their offerings to the lagoon and to connect with this ancient power center. The shaman said that although they must take additional steps before they could be initiated, they could be of great assistance in healing the planet. He explained that initiation is not necessarily a sign of spiritual development, but rather represents a readiness to assume responsibility for the planet and for serving humanity.

During initiation, the shaman helped us forge a link with an ancient lineage of knowledge. My understanding is that shamans believe this knowledge to be an information bank that exists in time but not in space, in the same world inhabited by the archetypal figures and the mythical deities. It became apparent to me that this link with the mythical world in some cases could even prove dangerous. Initiates must develop a strong connection with the earth so as not to lose themselves in the non-ordinary reality of the "overworld."

A number of our companions were upset that the shaman had not initiated them. They felt they had worked as hard as anyone else in the group, and they wanted to know what criteria the shaman had used for selecting those whom he had initiated. When I asked the shaman his reasons, he simply explained that some of the people were not ready, and that it would have been dangerous for them to undergo initiation.

As an example, don Eduardo pointed toward me and said that if I had been initiated five years earlier, I would in all likelihood have lost my interest in shamanism, for with my academic mentality I would have considered this a graduation ceremony and an indication that my work was done. Initiation, the shaman explained, is only the beginning. The greatest work still lies ahead of the initiate.

Months later, several of the members of our group would comment that they did indeed feel changed as a result of our journey. One claimed to feel a greater sense of responsibility toward healing others. Uta, the naturopathic physician, dedicated herself to the preservation of herbs and medicinal plants that were becoming extinct, and to reviving the use of these substances. Rainer, the German psychologist, became active in the organizing of conferences on the evolution of consciousness and wrote a book on the topic. Martin reported he was using the knowledge he acquired to help treat his patients.

The following day don Eduardo explained that initiation was a seed planted in our spirit which we now had to care for and cultivate. With care, it would take root and grow to great heights; if neglected, it would soon shrivel and die. The previous day's ceremony was the validation of a transformation that for one person had taken place while she was helping a companion carry a heavy bag. For another the transformation had taken place on the ruins in Machu Picchu. Initiation was basically a salute to the spirit of a person whose consciousness had been awakened.

Angelika, a filmmaker from Munich, commented, "I had a difficult struggle yesterday. I asked myself, If don Eduardo would have chosen me, would I have accepted? I was afraid of the responsibility involved as a result of the initiation. Would I have to come back to Peru every year to learn more? Would I have to change my lifestyle? I didn't know whether I could change my profession. I was confused about all of this. Then when I was not chosen, I was very sad but after a while I thought, no, it's all right like this. He knows that I'm not ready for it. And I was relieved."

The shaman believes that initiations are taking place all the time. Initiations can occur on the way to the supermarket or on top of the Himalayas. And the most powerful initiations, don Eduardo explained, are bestowed from the hands of masters who work directly from the "overworld." These initiations may occur in our dreams or during meditation, or may take us by surprise at times when we least expect them. But in the final analysis we make the choice to be initiated ourselves. While most of us wanted to take the steps that would lead to knowledge and power, few of us wanted to assume responsibility for the tribe, for the planet, and for the evolution of all life and consciousness. Don Eduardo explained that if newly initiated shamans did not cultivate the seeds of knowledge that had been planted in them, they would suffer and struggle much harder than a person who had not been initiated.

The Dance of the Four Winds

The following morning don Eduardo invited us to his home to witness the preparation of the San Pedro mixture. He explained that shamans throughout the world use sacred plants to open their vision. The substance's chief ingredients are a cactus and herbs that suspend ordinary states of consciousness.

"In Peru, the San Pedro has always been boiled," don Eduardo explained. "But it is also used raw by some shamans. For us, it has to be cooked for seven hours exactly so that it loses five of its ingredients. But two very important mescaline-like compounds remain. In the *huacos,* the ancient ceramics, you find male and female shamans holding the San Pedro cactus in their left hand while reciting their prayers. The San Pedro serves to connect one with the nature spirits, as well as with the great masters of the past and the spirits that protect certain sacred places. In addition to San Pedro, the ritual drink contains a number of other sacred herbs from the mountains, and from very special lagoons, the *hilcas.* One of these we call 'misha,' and another is the 'condor.' The spirits of all these herbs act together, purifying and smoothing the visions."

At ten o'clock that evening we gathered before the Temple of the Moon, where for millennia shamans have brought their apprentices to experience the "overworld." Shamans say that one should settle for nothing short of the direct experience of the Great Spirit. One can understand their conflict with the Roman Catholic priests who insisted that an intermediary was needed between individuals and God.

Two of don Eduardo's sons, also apprentices of the shaman, had prepared a circle of fire nearly twenty-five feet in diameter in front of the shaman's mesa. Don Eduardo said that the fire circle was a "safe space" be-

tween our physical world and the "overworld." Sitting
behind his mesa, with all of his power objects and staffs
before him, don Eduardo began to shake his rattle and
sing to the four winds to join us for tonight's ceremony.
He then took one of his swords, the "sword of fire," and
stepped inside the fire circle. To my astonishment, he
began to make aerial cartwheels, ritual leaps along the
four directions, cutting the energy fields that hold our
material reality together, cutting the connections with
the East, North, South, and West. The legends say that
in doing so a shaman risks his life—for if he loses control
or becomes distracted, he may be lost in the realm between the worlds. We were surprised by don Eduardo's
agility and how, despite weighing more than two hundred
pounds, he was able to leap through the air so gracefully.

The shaman explained that in the Dance of the Four
Winds we would connect with the four directions of the
"overworld." Two at a time, we stepped into the circle
and received a power staff. Beginning at the west, we
danced around the circle, spinning through the air when
we reached one of the cardinal points to unwind from
our material reality and reorient ourselves to the four
directions of the world of the spirit. When we finished
the dance we came back to the mesa and returned the
shaman's power staffs. He blew a mixture of sweet herbs
and alcohol from his *seguro* onto our hands, giving each
one of us a quartz crystal to maintain our connection to
him, to his teachers, and to this place of power.

Afterward we walked to the Temple of the Moon, to
pay our respects to the master buried there. Two members of our group were appointed "guides," and es-
corted us through a river of fog that suddenly appeared
between us and the temple. For many of us, the visit to
the Temple of the Moon was like returning to a home we
had not been in for millennia.

The new shamans believe that the initiates of don

Eduardo and other healers can play an important role in using this shamanic wisdom to bring more sanity to our world. But one does not have to be an initiate to learn from shamanic traditions. Initiation implies responsibility, and there are many ways in which we all could be more responsible for our Mother Earth. Industrial growth depends upon taking fossil fuels from the earth; from the shamanic point of view, these resources are to be borrowed and must be returned. It takes a few decades to ruin an inch of topsoil; it takes at least a century to return it. It takes a few hours to burn a forest, but it requires centuries for forests to grow back. Each of us can seek guidance from our dreams, from communal dialogue, and from solitary and group visions to take responsibility for the care of our Earth, for our atmosphere, our water supply, our soil, our forests, and our wildlife. It is estimated that over a dozen species disappear from the Earth every few days. The shaman views all life as interdependent; the loss of these species portends our own diminution and is a loss of part of our very selves.

The shamanic sensibility need not be restricted to shamans. The shaman encourages communities to assist individuals who are in need, whether they are sick, dispirited, disenfranchised, or alienated. We lack similar institutions and personnel in our modern societies, yet any of us can assume our portion of the shaman's role, that of steward of the Earth. When we muster the courage to marshal our inner forces, we can make a healing difference in our world.

PART III

From Primitive Myths to Planetary Healing

Strictly speaking, the term "shaman" should be applied only to practitioners in hunting, gathering, and/or fishing tribes. Don Eduardo Calderon and the practitioners we describe in this section (e.g., Rolling Thunder, Maria Sabina) are actually "shaman/healers" because they are members of sedentary communities. When a group of people settles down, the shaman's religious functions are gradually transferred to a priest as a creed becomes institutionalized and as dogma evolves. However, the shaman/healer is still turned to when a magical spell is required (for the hunt or for warfare) or when someone becomes ill, and altered states of consciousness are still used in hexing, diagnosing, and curing. Eventually, a sorcerer assumes the practice of magic and a diviner or medium specializes in altered states. "Healers" remain to treat the sick—but generally without the "astral flight" or the spirit consultations that characterized the shaman and the shaman/healer.

This section describes the development of magical and religious practitioners throughout history and explains how their private beliefs and visions became embedded in the cultural myths of a social group. You will have the opportunity to read about contemporary shaman/healers (whom we will call "shamans" for purposes of simplification), and how they differ from diviners, spiritists, and mediums. You will also be shown how to construct a "model" of healing, and we will contrast the allopathic model with a shamanic model. You will observe that contemporary shamanic models of healing typically interface with allopathic medicine and that shamans even

147

integrate allopathic medicine into their own worldview. Thus, there is little justification for anyone in a Western cultural setting to abandon allopathic medical care, even though it may be supplemented by practices based on "holistic" or "alternative" models of health and healing.

To some people, the world views of the allopathic physician and the native pactitioner seem irreconcilable, but in the chapters that follow, you will see that they can actually complement each other. For example, there are many illnesses that cannot be treated effectively by Western medicine but are routinely handled by shamans, mediums, and folk healers. On the other hand, there are victims of illnesses that baffle indigenous healers but are effectively cared for by allopathic physicians.

When Lynn V. Andrews, author of *Jaguar Woman,* completed her seven-year apprenticeship with Agnes Whistling Elk, the Cree medicine woman told her to write a book that would give away what she had learned. We have attempted to follow this example in *Healing States.* As you finish this book, we hope that you will be motivated to adopt those aspects of shamanic consciousness that appeal to you. How can you discover elements in your life that you consider to be truly sacred? How can you take better care of your health? How can you take better care of your neighbor? How can you take better care of the earth? Shamans are caretakers and represent a devotion to service that needs to be revived and maintained if the torn fabric of our culture is to be mended and transformed.

Chapter 12

Shamanic Ritual, Myth, and Medicine

Rolling Thunder

The first shaman with whom either of us had spent any considerable amount of time was Rolling Thunder, the Cherokee-born practitioner who eventually became well-known throughout North America and Europe.[1]

When the two of us visited Rolling Thunder's home in Carlin, Nevada, in 1974, he suggested that we hold a dance. During the summer months there is little rain in the desert, but Rolling Thunder stated that before such a dance it would be helpful if there were a brief shower to settle the dust. He added that after the dance, there should be a stronger rain to wash away the tracks of the dancers.

At sunset, we climbed into three cars and headed for an abandoned ranch a few miles away. The stars were shining brightly and there was not a cloud in sight. Three deer stood by the side of the road, glimpsed our caravan, and took off in a trot for the hills. Just a few seconds had elapsed, but when we looked at the sky again we observed small, puffy clouds gathering in front of us. A few minutes later we turned on the windshield wipers. The shower stopped as we arrived at the dancing ground. There were no puddles; the water had merely settled the dust.

We danced for hours as Rolling Thunder's "spiritual warriors" played drums and sang traditional songs. Rolling Thunder taught us the Snake Dance which is often used in healing ceremonies. The sky was still clear as we finished our dancing, but on the way to the cars, dark clouds gathered over the clearing. Thunder began to crack, there was lightning close by, and a heavy rain poured down as we ran the last few yards to our automobiles. Rolling Thunder remarked, "It's not good to leave our prints behind. We don't want the white folks to think that a bunch of savages and hippies were conducting some kind of pagan ceremony."

To some of the dancers it seemed as if Rolling Thunder had caused the rains to come before and after the dance. To Rolling Thunder, however, it was a matter of aligning himself with natural laws. The Swiss psychologist Carl Jung used the word "synchronicity" to refer to coincidences which contain some apparent meaning. Synchronicities are quite common in the world of the shaman, for whom time does not always travel in a straight line and for whom cause and effect are sometimes combined.

A Physical Healing

Another of these synchronicities occurred during our visit. A few nights before our arrival, Spotted Fawn, Rolling Thunder's wife, had seen a movie on television starring Corinne Calvet, a film actress. Just before we began our journey to Nevada, Calvet decided to make the trip with us. She had been bothered by abdominal pain, and had seen several physicians, but they simply prescribed painkilling drugs. Calvet requested assistance, and Rolling Thunder gave the matter considerable thought. The coincidental showing of the movie on television was, for him, a "sign" that a healing ceremony would be appropriate to the natural course of events.

Rolling Thunder had the impression that Calvet's pain was long-standing and severe; he announced that he would require assistance in the healing ceremony. He told us that we could help him, but first we would have to undergo "purification" in a sweat lodge ceremony.

Along with Rolling Thunder, three of his "spiritual warriors," and two of our male friends, we took off our clothes and entered a wickiup, a domelike structure constructed of saplings bent and tied together over which animal hides had been draped. A shallow pit had been dug in the center and filled with red-hot rocks. As Rolling Thunder sprinkled water on the hot rocks, an explosive hiss was followed by a wave of intense heat that enveloped our naked bodies. We took turns adding water and the heat increased until we thought our skin was on fire. With every breath, this fire seemed to extend to our lungs. We realized that we could not fight the heat. We had to receive the heat and ride with it.

Once we had made terms with the heat, we felt a peaceful sensation of "oneness." This unity extended to the group, and to nature itself. We chanted, prayed, and sang as the sweat poured from our bodies, purging us of any anxiety, worries, and concerns that would prevent us from participating fully in the forthcoming healing session.

According to custom, if one person leaves the wickiup, everyone has to leave because the circle has been broken. So we were under intense social pressure to accommodate to the heat. In retrospect, this was a major factor in the transcendental experience that both of us

151

had during the sweat lodge ceremony, where after nearly two hours we felt we could "hear" and "feel" the spirits of the ancestors that Rolling Thunder was calling. Eventually, however, one of the "spiritual warriors" could not endure any further heat and rolled back the hide flap which served as a door. The rest of us followed him out of the wickiup, showered, dressed, and reassembled in a circle around a campfire. Corinne Calvet was seated in a chair at one end of the circle.

Rolling Thunder instructed us to begin the Snake Dance (taught to us earlier in our visit) around the campfire. In the meantime, he worked with Calvet using raw meat, an eagle claw, and feathers, and ended by spitting something into a pail after sucking on her skin to "purify" her body and withdraw the pain. That night she went to bed exhausted but the next morning, upon awakening, she felt a complete absence of pain, which did not return, even weeks later after she had returned to her home.

A Psychological Healing

In 1979 I (Krippner) paid a return visit to Rolling Thunder. During the visit, the shaman asked me to hypnotize a young Indian man who was severely alcoholic and who had come to Meta Tante ("Go in Peace," the spiritual community founded by Rolling Thunder) seeking help. Rolling Thunder, who strictly enforced a rule prohibiting alcohol and other drugs at the encampment, had placed the afflicted man on a diet to "purify" his body and to prepare him for a healing ceremony.

I thought I would meet William—the Indian seeking help—before the ceremony so that I could determine which type of hypnosis would be best suited for him. However, he worked in town and was not available until the ceremony began. In fact, when I arrived at the campfire, he was already there, seated with some four dozen other members of the community. Drumming, chanting, and singing proceeded for about ninety minutes, and I suspected that the chanting and the music had already induced an altered state of consciousness in William and his friends.

When the drumming stopped, I was told to begin the hypnosis. I simply asked William to relax and imagine what it felt like for him to crave alcohol. When he indicated that he had been able to recreate this feeling, I asked him to transform the feeling into an image of some type. He reported that he could visualize a horrible monster that was intent on destroying him.

I reminded William that there were about fifty people around the campfire who cared for him very much and who would like to assist him. I told him that they would give him a gift and that he would be able to imagine it. Almost immediately William said that he "saw" a bow and arrow being given to him.

Remarking that the gift reflected his native American heritage, I told William that he could now kill the monster. He imagined shooting an arrow into its heart; the monster collapsed.

I led William through a relaxation exercise to prepare him for the next step of the process. Then I asked him what healthy beverages were among his favorites and he responded with a list of fruit juices and herbal teas. I had him imagine drinking one of these and enjoying it very much. I then suggested to him that whenever he craved alcohol he could turn the craving into a monster, shoot it with the bow and arrow, and drink (in reality or in his imagination) some juice or tea to quench his thirst. I suggested that the more often he went through the procedure, the more success he would have.

When I sat down, Rolling Thunder emerged, dressed in a white buckskin suit and a feather headdress. Before proceeding with his part of the ceremony, Rolling Thunder asked the group if it had heard the hooting of an owl. The group members affirmed that they had, and Rolling Thunder commented that this was a symbol of death or transformation. Thus, William was engaged in a life-and-death struggle with alcohol, his nemesis. Rolling Thunder added that the owl had hooted seven times. Seven is a lucky number for Native Americans, hence William's chances to win the battle were quite good. In fact, William left Meta Tante the following year, and at last report, was still sober.

Was synchronicity at work again? Did an owl actually hoot? If so, did it hoot seven times? I did not recall because I was intent upon leading William through the guided imagery process. But in the final analysis, the important lesson is that Rolling Thunder had used a purported synchronistic event in a dramatic manner to mobilize William's self-healing capacities within a context of tribal support. Shamans are highly imaginative people who often perceive connections between inner and outer events that escape those around them. Whether the connections are projected ("read into" a situation) or whether they reflect underlying structures of reality is a matter of conjecture. Synchronicity involves an inner psychological event that matches an external observable event; imagination probably plays an important role in establishing this connection.

In both of these healing sessions, Rolling Thunder poked his client's skin with an eagle feather until there was a noticeable wincing of discomfort. Rolling Thunder placed his mouth over that point and proceeded to cup the area with his hands, suck it with his mouth, and spit copious amounts of a dark red fluid into a pail. He explained that this was another "purification" procedure. The fluid was later taken to a wooded area and buried.

This cupping and sucking ritual is common among

many shamanic practitioners and some observers are under the impression that the client's impure blood is being withdrawn. Rolling Thunder says only that the fluid represents the client's illness, and that the ritual is necessary for health to be restored. In actuality, the fluid may be tobacco juice or some other type of liquid held in the shaman's mouth before the ceremony. On a few occasions, tests have indicated that the fluid is actually blood. Sometimes it is animal blood, swallowed in a bladder which is broken with the gastrointestinal muscles at the appropriate time. However, it can also be the blood of the shaman—produced either by severely biting the cheek or by an effort of self-regulation which evokes internal bleeding and vomiting the blood. Tobacco juice, we suspect, would be much easier and just as dramatic.

María Sabina

Another well-known shaman deeply involved with a world view including synchronicity was María Sabina, the Mazatec Indian *sabia* (or "wise one") of Mexico. In 1980, I (Krippner) visited her and held two interviews with her about her life mission. Her calling as a healer, she reported, dated back to an apparition of death she had during her sister's illness. She claimed that she saw a dark figure near her sister's side and became deeply concerned. Through prayer, she purportedly met spiritual beings who gave her guidance on how she could heal her sister. Her lessons involved the use of the "sacred mushrooms" (e.g., *Psiloscybe mexicana*) which she referred to as *los niños santos* ("the holy children").

From her adolescence until after the death of her second husband, doña María's use of the mushrooms was sporadic because of the prohibition against sexual activity before their ingestion. However, during her first few years of using them, she became convinced that the mushrooms gave wisdom, cured illness, and represented the blood and flesh of Jesus Christ. Indeed, there is an oral tradition of a fair-haired man-god, Quetzalcoatl, who walked through Mexico healing the sick and teaching the doctrine of universal love. One of the many myths concerning Quetzalcoatl has to do with his gift of the sacred mushrooms—*teonancatl,* "the flesh of God" —to his people. As Quetzalcoatl walked through Mexico, the *teonancatl* would grow where his spittle fell and from the drops of blood he lost when thorns cut into his feet. When the Spaniards conquered Mexico, Roman Catholicism replaced the native religion. However, Christ and Quetzalcoatl were syncretized by Native Americans in many parts of the country.

In 1955 another possible example of synchronicity occurred when María Sabina had a mushroom-induced vision that strangers would visit her town seeking knowledge about the *teonancatl.* In the vision she was instructed to supply this knowledge, even though it meant breaking a secret tradition which went back over the centuries. Within a short period of time, R. Gordon Wasson, the mycologist (mushroom specialist), arrived with Allan Richardson, a photographer. They asked about the mushrooms and doña María answered their questions, after seeking confirmation of her vision with a municipal authority who agreed with her that this knowledge should be shared.

Wasson and Richardson were the first recorded outsiders to ingest mushrooms in a native ceremony. Wasson later wrote that the experience shook him to the very core of his being, that it was both profound and sacred.[2] Wasson described his experience for *Life* magazine, and it was not too long before many foreigners came to Huautla de Jiménez, not to be healed but to search for God. The Mazatec Indians had not eaten the mushrooms for such a purpose; their tradition held that the divine plant was to be used for highly specific reasons.[3]

Again, doña María had a synchronous vision. This time the omen was tragic. In her words, "I saw the entire life of my son Aurelio and his death and the face and the name of the man that was going to kill him and the dagger with which he was going to kill him, because everything had already been accomplished. The murder had already been committed, and it was useless for me to say to my son that he should look out because they would kill him. There was nothing to say." A group of townspeople were angered that María Sabina had revealed the mushroom tradition to outsiders. Not only was her son killed but her house and store were burned to the ground. Yet she claimed that even without the advice of the municipal authority, she would have revealed the secret to Wasson because the mushrooms had so instructed her.

Among the Mazatecs, there are three groups of people with alleged special powers. There are the sorcerers and witches—the *brujos* and *brujas*—who live somewhat apart from the community and sell their cures, spells, and hexes for a price. There are the *curanderos* and *curanderas*, the herbal healers. Finally, there are the *sabias* and *sabios*, the "wise ones" or shamans. María Sabina was a *curandera* for a while, working not with mushrooms but with herbs and offerings, using eggs and other materials for "spiritual cleansings." But among the Mazatecs, the power of both the herbalist and the sorcerer are thought to come from Chicon Nindo, the ancient Mazatec Lord of the Mountains. The power of the "wise one" is greater because it comes from Christ-Quetzalcoatl through the sacred mushrooms.

As word of doña María's power spread, sick and dispirited Indians came from various parts of the area to participate in her *veladas*—to eat *los niños santos* and

157

await their visions. They would sit in darkness while María Sabina clapped her hands, danced, and sang such verses as:

"Woman of good spirit am I . . . Hail, most holy Mary, oh Jesus Christ . . . Woman who waits am I, Woman who divines am I . . . For I am a daughter of Christ . . . Woman of justice am I, Woman of law am I, God knows me, The saints know me, Woman of the Southern Cross am I, Woman of the Star of God am I, For I go up to the sky. . . . "[4]

When doña María chanted, the spirits would supposedly come, as well as the figure of Christ. The spirits would handle practical matters such as dictating remedies to illnesses, the location of lost or stolen objects, and solutions to problems. They advised her on which herbs to find and how to use them, which saints or spirits to invoke, and what pilgrimages to make. Sometimes the client would vomit, supposedly ejecting malignant spirits from the body. The mushrooms might themselves cure chills, fevers, toothaches, and a variety of other maladies, or even rescue a benevolent spirit trapped by the spirit masters in the springs or the mountains.

Doña María's ceremonial liturgy does contain Roman Catholic elements but they are merely an overlay; at the core are the same ancient odes and psalms that were uttered by the high priests of Montezuma the Second before he was overthrown by Hernán Cortés in 1521. Until mind-altering plants were outlawed by the Spanish Inquisition, psychedelic effects were obtained from the peyote cactus and from certain varieties of morning glory seeds as well as from the mushrooms of the genus *Psilocybe* and, to a lesser extent, from the *Conocybe* and *Stropharia* varieties.[5] When the mushrooms were out of season, or when her supply of dried mushrooms was low, doña María used San Pedro tobacco, a member of the Solanaceae family which has mind-altering properties. Archeological evidence indicates that psychoactive plants were used in the New World some ten thousand years ago, and may be related to the shamanic use of Amanita muscaria mushrooms in Siberia and other portions of Eurasia.

María Sabina was born about 1894, and as she approached her ninth decade she had to forgo her nighttime rituals because of her fragile health. Shortly after my 1980 visit, word reached me that she had married for the third time and was engaged in preserving the mushroom tradition by actively teaching. Doña María died in 1985, ending a life filled with hardship and ecstasy, persecution and service.

One of her daughters had helped doña María pray and sing during the healing rituals but it was believed that she was not born with the destiny to become a "wise one." Like those of us who knew her, she is left with doña María's description of the cosmos in a way that includes synchronous events: "I saw . . . an immense clock that ticks, the spheres that go slowly around, and inside the stars, the earth, the entire universe, the day and the night, the cry and the smile, the happiness and the pain. He who knows to the end of the secret of the *teonancatl* can even see that infinite clockwork."[6]

Technicians of the Sacred

What do these people have in common that they attain the label of "shaman"? What characteristics does María Sabina share with Rolling Thunder? The noted ethnologist Mircea Eliade poetically described shamans as "technicians of the sacred" because they mediate between the world of mortals and the world of the spirits.[7]

Rolling Thunder, perhaps because of his contact with physicians and psychologists, speaks of "entering an altered state of consciousness" during many of his ceremonies and healing sessions. For doña María it was the mushrooms which altered consciousness. Both of these altered states are "lucid" in the sense that the shaman is aware during the experience and recalls the events later. In addition, the altered states are entered for a purpose; they assist the self-development of the practitioner or they assist clients or the community in some manner.

So we might say that shamans are men and women who are able to voluntarily alter their consciousness to enter "extraordinary reality" in order to obtain knowledge, power, and skills that can help or heal members of their tribe—the social group which confers and maintains their shamanic role. This definition can be rephrased in psychological terms. Shamans are tribal people who can self-regulate their attention so as to access information not ordinarily available, using it to ameliorate the physical or psychological condition of members of their social group. Shamans operate within a social context; a tribal group accepts them as "technicians of the sacred" and benefits from the information they purport to bring back from their voyages to the other world, or from their communication with spirit entities. In addition, most shamans are said to be able to harmonize with the forces of nature, evoking rain or sunshine, when called for, by a ceremony.

The Shaman's Role

In early hunting and gathering societies, survival was a day-by-day struggle. Not much time was available for reflection on the inner life. But when anyone recalled a dream, its contents were regarded as real, just as daily events were real. The dream world, of course, did not correspond exactly to the everyday world, and the notion developed that dreams took people to another world —not less real than the ordinary one but somewhat more puzzling. Shamans had explanations for that world; if an explanation made sense, helped sick people get well, or assisted hunters to find game, the shaman's social standing increased. If the shaman's attempts to placate the spirits, to heal the sick, or to keep the tribal hunters informed of the location of wild animals were not successful, the shaman was usually demoted, ridiculed, exiled, or even killed.

The first shamans must have been very clever people in order to ensure their position of influence in the tribe. They located medicinal herbs, and discovered new ones on a trial-and-error basis or by observing the eating habits of animals. They designed rituals to improve the perception of hunters and gatherers so they could more accurately locate game and food. Most important, they created rites of passage that facilitated the journey from birth to death, and developed procedures to allow members of their group to contact the sacred. Sometimes this involved mind-altering plants; at other times their rituals employed art, song, dance, storytelling, music, chanting —all essential components of tribal life.

In other words, shamans represent the world's oldest profession. Their roles probably varied from one society to another, but it is likely that they served a number of functions: artist, healer, magician, priest, psychotherapist, seer, storyteller. In so doing, they assisted the evolution of human consciousness. The trails blazed by the shamans were followed by other members of the tribe; their followers developed similar abilities and the cultural heritage soon began to include dream interpretation, artistic technology, medicinal knowledge, and religious rituals.

Shamans were also the world's first scientists. Their discoveries of medicinal and sacred plants were made through observation and trial-and-error, both honored scientific procedures. In addition, they probably experimented on themselves, another scientific practice. Their observations of astronomical events produced additional data, as is exemplified by a legend related by the Zuñi Indians of the southwest United States. According to this story, a shaman was told by the Sun, "Come to the edge of the village every morning and pray to me. At the end of the year when I come to the South, watch me closely. And in the middle of the year in the same month when I reach the farthest point on the right hand, watch me closely." During the next year, the shaman watched the sun but his calculations for the solstice were early by thirteen days. The following year he was twenty days early. The next year he was two days late. However, after eight years the shaman was able to time the turning of the sun exactly.[8]

Observations such as these were conducted in thousands of areas around the world and laid the foundations of modern science. They provided humankind with the first tangible clues that there was order in the universe, because these observations could be replicated hundreds of times and still yield uniform results. If the shamans did not produce reliable data, their role was endangered and their days of honor were numbered. Thus, humanity owes a massive debt to shamans for their pioneering work in the accumulation of knowledge and the development of human capabilities.

Chapter 13

Models of Shamanic Healing

Shamans became the world's first mythmakers and as such gave their tribes and villages a way to understand the world around them. These shamanic myths served four purposes. First, there was the psychological function of providing a marked pathway for carrying the individual through the various life stages from birth until death. Second, there was the sociological function of validating and enforcing a specific social and moral order. Third, there was the scientific function of providing some understandable and dependable explanation of nature and natural phenomena. Fourth, there was the spiritual function of linking waking consciousness with the vast mystery and wonder of the cosmos. As societies became more complex, the shamanic myths became interwoven into the fabric of culture itself. The later myths fulfilled three of the four functions, but they never were able to provide as dependable an explanation of natural phenomena as empirical science, and with the ascent of science we saw the decline of myth. However, science was never able to adequately encompass the other three functions, just as modern-day scientists, with all their technology, have been unable to match the ancient role of shamans as technicians of the sacred.

The Shaman, the Healer, and the Diviner

Our colleague Michael Winkelman has devoted several years to investigating the relationship between shamanic roles and social evolution, making an intensive study of forty-seven societies, both past and present.[1] Winkelman was struck by the clear emergence of four groups of practitioners in the domain of the sacred.* These four groups included the shaman (as well as the shaman-healer and healer), the priest, the malevolent practitioner (or sorcerer), and the diviner (or medium). Originally, in the early hunting and gathering societies, all of these roles were performed by shamans. They could serve as religious functionaries, divine the future, and cast hexes —especially against tribal enemies.

As tribes became more sedentary, there were instances where the healing functions were divided between the shaman and another person, or group of people. In the process, certain differences appeared. Whereas shamans showed little specialization, the healers were highly specialized, working with one specific group of procedures (e.g., herbal treatments or bone setting) or for one purpose (e.g., to heal sick animals). While the shaman's political power was great, it was generally informal, whereas Winkelman found that the healers occupied a specific place in the political hierarchy and often purchased their position. The shaman usually trained with an older shaman on a one-to-one basis or claimed to learn from the spirits in dreams or other altered states of consciousness. The healers, however, were typically taught in groups led by more experienced practitioners.

Winkelman found that the shaman focused more inten-

---

* There was also a secular domain, usually presided over by a king, queen, ruler, or chief.

sively upon issues such as weather control and ensuring success in the hunt, while the healers were preoccupied with birth, marriage, death, and other rites of passage. The shaman prophesied while in an altered state of consciousness but the healer divined the future by throwing bones, reading animal entrails, or using other mechanical methods. The shaman engaged in extremely profound alterations in consciousness such as out-of-body travel (the "astral flight"), but none of the healers in Winkelman's sample followed these practices.

When a tribe was at least semisedentary, devoted to agriculture to some extent, and characterized by a fair amount of political integration, the priest emerged as a separate practitioner. Priests and priestesses presided over religious functions, especially those marking important events in the life cycle, and in cosmological cycles (e.g., the seasons, the solstices); organized sacrifices and other rituals to placate and honor the gods; acquired considerable political power and economic status; and worked full-time at their tasks.

When a society achieved full social and political integration and became fully sedentary, the malevolent practitioner, or sorcerer, was added to the number of people with purported special abilities. Usually a part-time worker who lived somewhat apart from the rest of the social group, the sorcerer had low political and economic status. Both males and females took over this role.

Only when societies evolved to a higher level of political integration and became more dependent upon agricultural pursuits did the diviner emerge as an important practitioner. Primarily women, diviners often combined their domestic duties with their divinatory functions. Some of them were involved in healing, especially when spirits needed to be contacted. Like shamans, they entered altered states of consciousness; their specialty was not the "astral flight" but the incorporation of spirits. Like today's mediums, they rarely recalled what the spirit did or said while they were possessed; their bodies and voices were vehicles for higher powers.

Winkelman found a strong relationship between the number of special practitioners and a society's complexity. If there was one practitioner present, it was almost always a shaman or healer. If there were two present, one was always a shaman or healer and the other was either a priest or a malevolent practitioner. If three were present, one was always the shaman or healer, and the other two were generally the priest and the sorcerer. If the society was highly complex, the diviner was added and all four roles were filled by separate people.

Winkelman's distinction between shamans and healers was somewhat arbitrary, because there were more similarities than differences. It was an important one, however, because he found shamans only in societies with no social classes and little political integration.

Priests as well as healers were commonly found in sedentary, agricultural societies. No diviners were found among American Indian tribes; these, of course, were devoid of the high level of political organization typical of the societies that encourage the development of mediums. Perhaps mediumistic possession is only possible if the social group is able to provide a safe, protective milieu to support this surrender of self-awareness. Winkelman's study included Indian tribes, ancient Babylonia and Rome, the African Kung, and a number of Oriental social groups. His research illustrates how the shaman, over the millennia, has assisted in the evolution of culture and has also delegated his or her functions to other practitioners when the society displays the proper readiness.

Dimensions of Healing

Winkelman's study involved both past and present societies from all over the world. This book takes a more modest scope, with its focus upon shamans, healers, and mediums whom we have visited in North and South America. Rolling Thunder, for example, is a shaman who also performs healing and divining functions. He is an expert on herbs and on native American prophecies. He contacts spirits but does not incorporate them. During his "astral flights" he experiences flying with the eagle, his "totem bird," from whom he says he is constantly learning new skills.

María Sabina was a shaman in a society where healers (*curanderos* and *curanderas*) also function. In addition, doña María performed divinatory tasks. She claimed to speak with the Mazatec spirits and with the Christian saints. Her "astral flights" took her "up to the sky." As she remarked in one of her chants, "That's the way it looks when I go to heaven. They say it's like softness there. They say it's like land. They say it's like day. They say it's like dew."[2] While very poetic, María Sabina's description does not help us comprehend her healing abilities.

To better understand the way that native peoples conceptualize healing, it is important to compare their models with that of Western medicine. A model is simply an attempt to represent and explain reality. It is like a map—and like a map it may represent its territory quite well or rather poorly.

Miriam Siegler and Humphry Osmond have created a model of healing that contains twelve dimensions: diagnosis, cause of disease, client's behavior, goal, treatment, prognosis, suicide and death, role of the institution, role of healing personnel, client's rights and duties, families' rights and duties, and society's rights and duties.³ We will examine allopathy on these twelve dimensions, and then contrast it with a shamanic model of healing.

"Allopathy" is a term coined in the nineteenth century to describe medicinal treatment that "fights" disease because the drug and the causative agent are fundamentally "different." Diagnosis for the allopathic physician is a logical procedure; the information is gathered by questioning, observing, and testing. The physician usually shares some, but not necessarily all, of this information with the patient. The cause of the disease is natural rather than supernatural or magical; it is logically connected to signs and symptoms manifested by the patient. Usually, treatment is specific for each disease, but when a diagnosis is not known it may proceed by trial and error.

The goal of allopathic medicine is to restore the patient to health. If this is not possible, the disease must be prevented from getting worse, or at least circumscribed to protect society. Another ancillary goal reduces any blame that might be felt by the patient's relatives by conferring the "sick" role on the patient. Allopathy also seeks to accumulate medical knowledge so that more diseases can be cured and so that cures can become more effective. It is assumed that eventually every disease will have its cure. The treatment offered by allopathy may involve surgery and/or drugs. Nursing care is sometimes a part of the treatment. In each case, the treatment is specifically related to the disease and monitored according to the patient's behavior or response.

Prognosis, the forecast of the disease's course, is carried out by the physician and based on the diagnosis. The physician believes that the diagnosis limits the possible outcomes; he or she can offer hope but cannot promise a cure.

Suicide and death are to be avoided at all costs. Death

is seen as the failure of the treatment, or as the inevitable result of aging or of an illness that is unresponsive to the best treatment currently available.

The role of the institution is to serve as a place where virtually all patients are seen and where some patients are cared for during a short or long period of time. Patients do not "live" in an institution; they "stay" there until the treatment is completed.

The role of the healing personnel varies; the physician will treat the patients, nurses will care for them, and other staff members will sometimes rehabilitate them.

The patient's rights and duties are associated with the diagnosis. In each case, the patient has the right to be sick. The role of a sick person is assigned without blaming patients, except in cases in which the illness is related to self-destructive behavior. Patients have the right to be informed about their illness and their progress. They have the right to special care. They have the duty to try to get well, and to seek help in order to get well. Once medical help is offered, the patients have the duty to cooperate with those offering the help.

The family's rights and duties interface with those of the patient. Family members have the right to sympathy and the right to receive information about the illness. They have the duty to collaborate with the treatment and the obligation not to obstruct it in any way.

Society's rights and duties include the right to be protected from people who, because of their illness, are a danger to others. Society has a duty to provide medical care in one form or another (although some societies take this duty more seriously than do others).

Recent criticism of allopathic medicine centers around various aspects of this model. Some claim that diagnosis and treatment are often impersonal and incomplete. Typically, the patient lacks any input into the decision-making process. Overuse of drugs and surgery, and increasing malpractice by physicians, are alleged. There is an unequal allocation of healing services in many parts of society. The patients and their families often are restrained in the choice of controversial treatments in cases of serious illnesses. On the one hand, there is no doubt that Western medicine has produced many benefits, especially in the fight against epidemics and infectious disease. On the other hand, dissatisfaction with Western medicine's approach to cancer, heart disease, and other ailments has led many people to turn to "holistic" medicine* or even to such nonallopathic approaches as chiropractic, homeopathy, naturopathy, and osteopathy.

The Pima Indians—A Model of Shamanic Healing

Among the Pima Indians of Arizona, diagnosis is accomplished by the shaman, whose main task is to make the person aware of his or her illness after deciding what type of sickness is involved and how it was caused.[4] The Pima shamans differentiate between two different types of affliction. The first type is futile to treat. Examples include certain cases of broken bones, constipation, indigestion, infant deformities, mental retardation, and venomous bites. These conditions either are seen as permanent or are thought to improve without treatment.

The second type consists of curable ailments. One

---

* "Holistic" approaches to medicine generally include a consideration of the "whole person" (body, mind, emotions, and spirit), bringing the patient and the patient's family into the treatment process, stressing prevention of disease through healthy attitudes and lifestyles, and using "natural" therapeutic interventions (such as fasting, dieting, exercise, positive thinking, self-regulation of body functions) before resorting to drugs and surgery. These approaches, of course, have much in common with the native healing traditions practiced by Rolling Thunder, María Sabina, Eduardo Calderon and the other shamans and healers we have met.

such ailment is "wandering sickness," caused by impurities that "wander" through the body. Another is "staying sickness," caused by improper behavior toward "objects of power" such as buzzard feathers, clouds, coyotes, deer, jimson weed, and roadrunner birds. One "stays sick" a long time when afflicted by these ailments. When the Europeans arrived it was observed that they did not fall victim to "staying sickness" when they violated power objects. Did this observation challenge the model? Not at all. The Pima concluded that the white settlers did not contract these illnesses because to them the objects were not sacred. "Staying sickness" did not affect other Native American tribes either, the Pima observed; they also noticed that it did not affect animals who transgressed the rules.

The Pima consider the patient's behavior important for several reasons. The patient's body is considered to be the repository for a lifetime's acquisition of sickness-causing potentials. It is the task of the shaman to determine which of these potentials are involved in the illness. Some people are more susceptible than others to noxious substances (heat, pus, diseases caught from other people). When the Pima were told about the germ theory of disease, this knowledge strengthened rather than weakened their model. Germs simply became another of the noxious substances held to cause "wandering sickness."

The goal of Pima healing is both preventive and prescriptive; health is to be maintained while both "wandering" and "staying" sicknesses are to be cured. The treatment for "wandering sickness" is typically herbs and (since the arrival of the Europeans) medicines. The treatment for "staying sickness" involves chanting, singing, sand painting (placing the patient on a decorated area where "healing energies" can be absorbed), applying crystals and blowing the harmful spirits away from the patient, and sucking the offending spirits from the patient's body. The prognosis is hopeful if the treatment is appropriate, prompt, and carried out with sufficient power. If the treatment is not carried out appropriately, death or continued illness may occur. Suicide is a possible result of succumbing to the temptation of evil spirits.

The role of the institution is to serve as the setting for the healing. Even physicians' offices and hospitals can be used for some types of "wandering sicknesses." The shaman may also turn "wandering sickness" over to Piman healers who are herbal specialists. For "staying sicknesses," the healing environment is usually an out-of-doors setting such as a campfire where the shaman attempts to block or exterminate the disease.

The role of healing personnel depends on the ailment; the herbal healer treats "wandering sickness" and the shaman treats "staying sickness." Physicians and nurses can treat germ-related "wandering sicknesses." Germs are conceived as tiny particles that wander through the world, enter humans, and manifest themselves as symptoms; the shaman does not treat these problems because they can be handled by others. There are at least forty types of dangerous power objects, each with its own "staying sickness" (e.g., "horned toad sickness," "eagle sickness"). Unlike shamans who journey to cosmological realms (such as the "overworld," "middle earth," and the "lower world"), Piman shamans concentrate on the potentials inside the patient's body. Spirits are contacted, but basically as the ultimate means for solving the patient's problems.

Piman patients have the right to treatment, the duty to cooperate with the healer, and, in the case of "staying sickness," the duty to refrain from further violation of power objects. The family has the right to request treatment for its indisposed members and the duty to keep from offending the power objects, because not only

172

might they fall prey to a "staying sickness" but their children might as well. Society has the right to have healing practitioners (shamans, herbalists, physicians, nurses) available and the duty to obey the spiritual laws so that its people will be protected from plagues and epidemics. Thus the Piman model of healing is part of Piman cultural mythology which holds that some objects and species are endowed with dignity at the time of creation. To behave improperly toward eagles, horned toads, coyotes, and the like is to offend the natural order of things. Disease is a logical consequence of this disruption, and the shaman attempts to restore the natural order.

Allopathy and Piman healing are two models that address the twelve dimensions necessary for a complete therapeutic approach. The flexibility and resiliency of the Piman model can be seen by its accommodation to the discovery that Europeans and other Indian tribes did not succumb to "staying sickness," as well as to the theory of germs. There are literally hundreds of major models of healing around the globe, some of them new and some of them ancient. Indeed, allopathy is used to treat no more than 15 to 20 percent of the peoples of the earth.

Chapter 14

Healing and Ecstatic
States of Trance

An altered state of consciousness for a given individual is one in which he or she experiences a shift from ordinary psychological functioning, i.e., displays or feels a different pattern of perceptions, thoughts, and emotions. This change is often apparent to outside observers who notice changes in the individual's behavior. One pioneering investigation demonstrated the effects on consciousness of rhythmic drumming. Subjects were exposed to the rhythm of a drum similar to the deerskin drums used by many North American Indian shamans. Major brainwave changes were observed when the frequencies were changed (for example, from two beats to four beats per second). The subjects reported a wide variety of visual and auditory imagery with their eyes closed. The altered state was enhanced by exertion (with resulting adrenaline secretion), hyperventilation (deep and rapid breathing), and fasting (which produces hypoglycemia). All of these factors are present in various Native American Spirit Dances and Sun Dances. The drumming rhythms are most effective if they corresponded to the theta brain rhythms (four to seven cycles per second), a rhythm characteristic more of Haitian voodoo than of North American Indian drumming.[1]

North American Indians have typically combined drumming and dancing with other procedures to alter consciousness. Their success is attested to by the notorious 1884 Canadian law against ceremonial dancing and the banning of the Sioux Sun Dance by U.S. governmental authorities, also in the 1880s. Purportedly, the regulations were put into effect because of the "uncivilized" self-torture often observed in their ceremonies, but the real reason was the recognition of the inherent nationalistic potentials of the rites.

In 1951 the Canadian law was removed and shamans traveled among the West Coast Salish tribes to revive the Spirit Dance. The reconstitution of this ceremony helped many alienated and dispirited Indians achieve a positive cultural identity. Shamans referred to these problems as "spirit illnesses." People who are thought to suffer from "spirit illnesses" submit to a ritual in which they are symbolically clubbed to death by the shaman. They are then symbolically resurrected and "reborn" after going through a womblike experience in the seclusion of a dark tent, sometimes for several days. With the assistance of Indian spirits and power animals which appear in visions, they find their own "spirit song," often in a vision or a dream. They emerge from the tent, accompanied by the singing and drumming of musicians, run through the woods, are bathed in a smokehouse, and receive power from the shaman, who blows his breath into the "newborn person," bringing him or her fully back to life.[2]

The Sioux Sun Dance was revived in the 1960s and is held yearly. The participants claim to have been directed to the dance through dreams and visions. They are tutored by shamans and endure a regimen of fasting and thirsting before the Sun Dance begins. Not only are

175

Sioux Indians represented, but other Plains tribes attend as well. The initiates purify themselves in the sweat lodge, pass the pipe around their circle, then enter the arena in a procession led by the Sun Dance chiefs and the bearer of the sacred buffalo skull. They alternately charge toward and retreat from the central pole representing the Tree of Life, a source of cosmic power.

The first dancer is tied to the central pole by rawhide ropes fastened to skewers which the Sun Dance chiefs slide through the outer layer of skin of the initiate's chest after making incisions with a ceremonial knife. The devotee blows his eagle-bone whistle and holds a power staff for protection while dancing and tugging for hours until the flesh is broken. Receiving a vision, he falls exhausted and is placed in such a position that his head points to the Tree of Life.

Some dancers may forgo the skewers but may dance until the vision is received. They are then lifted from their feet and are thrown to the ground by what they perceive as a jolt of power. This movement is typical in shamanism, and is reminiscent of the Siberian Tungus term "saman"—meaning "one who is excited, moved, heated, and raised"—from which "shaman" is derived. These dancers, too, are placed with their heads toward the central pole, the source of the power which now pervades them. It is felt that the dancers' spirits have left the body for a journey to the other world. Some time later, the dancer revives, inspirited and transformed.

The Spirit Dance and other shamanic ceremonies of this nature are important healing rituals. Their revival also suggests that social healing and integration are taking place. From a psychological point of view, there are several contributing factors, including altered states of consciousness in which this integration can occur. These include conditions of increased external stimulation and motor hyperactivity alternating with reduced external stimulation and motor hypoactivity. There are other factors, such as the power of suggestion, the power of the ritual, the imaginary or real pain, and the social support that permits and encourages the healing song or vision to emerge. It is also likely that endorphins and other brain chemicals are released which enable the initiate to bear the pain and strain while experiencing euphoria and ecstasy.[3]

Dreams and Healing States

Dreams represent a less dramatic but more universal altered state of consciousness in which healing can take place or in which diagnosis can occur. Many shamans are called to their profession through dreams. Dreams of dead relatives are held to mark one's call to shamanism among the Wintu and Shasta tribes of California. Among two other California tribes, the Diegunos and Luisanos, future shamans supposedly can be identified as early as nine years of age on the basis of their dreams. Among several other American Indian tribes, initiatory dreams contain such creatures as bears, deer, eagles, and owls that instruct the dreamer to draw upon their power and begin shamanic training.

Among Peru's Cashinatua Indians, the tribal hunters request herbalists to give them medicines to keep them from dreaming because they believe that the process interferes with their skill in hunting. Cashinatua shamans, however, believe that the more dreams they have, the greater their power will become; therefore, they develop methods to "pursue dreams." The Iroquois of North America had a sophisticated theory that dreams represented one's hidden desires. Thus they contained clues for the shamans to decipher as to what could be done to restore a person's health by fulfilling the desires in a manner consistent with the tribal social structure. A yearly ceremony was held in which everyone was required to relate important dreams. This was another socially approved manner in which unconscious wishes could be released.

Unpleasant dreams are held to be causes of disease among the Maricopa Indians, bringing on colds, diarrhea, and aches. Paviotso Indian children can become ill if their parents' dreams are unfavorable or if unpleasant dreams occur to visitors in the house. Shamanic intervention is asked for in either event to halt the effect. The Taulipang shamans in the Caribbean are called upon to interpret dreams of tribal members. When the Cuna Indians of Panama have dreams of an impending illness or disaster, the shaman administers a variety of cures to prevent the problem from occurring. The Cuna shaman may employ a unique out-of-body experience for purposes of diagnosis—leaving his own body and entering the body of the client to inspect possible physical difficulties. Thus the shaman may use his or her own dreams, and those of the tribe, for many purposes: to determine his or her shamanic calling, to diagnose and treat illness, to create songs and dances, to discover new charms and cures, to identify criminals, to locate lost objects, to plan military campaigns, and to name newborn children.[4]

Their frequent use of dreams underscores the shaman's status as a unique person in his or her tribe. As a result of physical, psychological, and/or social factors, the shaman was highly imaginative, recalling dreams more frequently than other tribal members and dealing with them creatively. This imaginative ability included identification of synchronous events, the talent for telling stories incorporating cultural myths, the power of visual imagery, and the susceptibility for entering culturally sanctioned altered states of consciousness quickly, deeply, yet with some degree of lucidity and control.

If such an individual were to become an integral part

of the society, he or she would need to serve a social function. She may not have been content with the pre-scribed female role. He may have lacked the physical dexterity to be a valuable hunter, or the leadership skills to become a chief. But probably neither the hunter nor the chief possessed the sensitivity and insight required to tend the sick, contact the spirits, or predict changes in the weather. These were tasks for a "technician of the sacred," and this was the role that these highly imagina-tive individuals assumed if they were to survive.

Later, many of their functions would be assumed by the priest, the diviner, and the sorcerer. Later still, with the institutionalization of religions, private visions were discouraged or even punished; sacred functions became the province of the priest, while techniques of magic were the province of the sorcerer. The diviner still main-tained a direct contact with the spirit world, but assumed no responsibility for the contents of his or her utterings, ascribing them to whatever spirits took possession at that moment. The diviner usually claimed not to remem-ber the messages once he or she returned to ordinary consciousness, again disowning much of the experience.

We live in a world alienated from its sacred dimension. Perhaps the healing states developed by shamans and diviners through the centuries still have something to offer not only their individual clients, but entire societies as well.

Shamans and the Ecstatic Trance

Some anthropologists have defined the term "shaman" very broadly and would not hesitate to use it to encom-pass the Brazilian spiritists as well as individuals like Eduardo Calderon and María Sabina. Our case for sepa-rating shamans from diviners (or mediums) can be briefly summarized as follows: Diviners emerged later in community evolution than did shamans, who are associated with hunting and gathering societies and semisedentary societies with little political integration or social stratification. Shamans enter into a variety of altered states of consciousness, one of which involves interaction with or incorporation of spirits. Even so, the shaman has a great degree of control of the state, is "lucid" during the state, and remembers the experience when it is over. The diviner's incorporation (or possession) states are usually uncontrolled, or at least less controlled, and the claim of amnesia for the state is frequently made. Admittedly, the distinction between shamans and diviners is not clearcut and some practitioners defy easy classification.

Some researchers have taken the position that shamans and diviners are schizophrenic. These writers point to the bizarre emotional experiences which often typify a shaman's calling: the initiate may hear voices, see visions, and manifest what many psychiatrists and psychologists would term "hallucinations" and "delusions." Sometimes these manifestations are terrifying; reports of hearing the shrieks of demons or seeing one's body torn apart are not uncommon. The shamanic call is also likened to a psychotic break in that both reflect the inability to solve the practical problems of existence, taking an eccentric, idiosyncratic path instead.

The American Psychiatric Association identifies the thought content of schizophrenics as being overtly negative in tone, with "paranoia" being present in about half of all schizophrenics. This involves "delusions that are often multiple, fragmented, or bizarre (i.e., patently absurd, with no possible basis in fact). Simple persecutory delusions involving the belief that others are spying on, spreading false rumors about, or planning harm to the individual are quite common."[5] In addition, paranoia involves "the belief or experience that thoughts that are not one's own and are inserted into one's mind ('thought insertion'); that thoughts have been removed from one's head ('thought withdrawal') or that one's feelings, impulses, thoughts or actions are not one's own but are imposed by some external force (delusions of 'being controlled')."[6]

Even the most superficial examination of the accounts of shamans about their experiences indicates that these negative, involuntary themes of intrusion are absent. Further, the shaman is typically able to differentiate between ordinary conscious experience and the altered state. Shamans can also tell the difference between inner and outer experience. Schizophrenics can make neither distinction easily. The shaman can master and control an altered state; the shaman can and does differentiate and not confuse the outer world and the inner world.

Psychiatrists also describe schizophrenic hallucinations: "By far the most common are auditory, frequently involving voices the individual perceives as coming from outside his or her head. The voices may be familiar and often make insulting statements. Command hallucinations may be obeyed, at times creating danger for the individual or for others."[7]

The schizophrenic is victimized by these voices, mercilessly criticized and mocked by them, and has no control over the hallucinations. By contrast, the experience of the shaman is usually visual. When it is auditory, the voices of the spirits are usually of a positive, helpful, healing nature. The advice given by spirits is willfully sought out by the shaman. Furthermore, the "vision quest" for obtaining direction on the part of the North American shaman may involve "seeing" spirits or power animals, but the dialogues with these entities do not resemble the auditory hallucinations common to the schizophrenic.

Psychiatry uses the term "magical thought" when an individual believes that his or her thoughts, words, or actions might be linked with a specific outcome in some way that defies ordinary laws of cause and effect. In other words, the schizophrenic believes in synchronistic events. In this case, there is a definite similarity between schizophrenics and shamans. But it should be recalled that people in primitive cultures generally engage in "magical thinking," as do children, traditional Eastern philosophers, psychotherapists influenced by Carl Jung, and others who accept synchronicity as a possible natural phenomenon. This type of thought may be immature or it may be fanciful thinking, but it is not limited to schizophrenics.

Another refutation of the argument that shamans are schizophrenics comes from the results of personality testing. In one such study, twelve Apache Indian shamans were given Rorschach inkblot tests.* The shamans' responses did not indicate the presence of schizophrenia, or even that they had recovered from schizophrenia. In general, they were psychologically healthier than other members of their society, had a greater capacity to test reality, and a better ability to use their imagination.† They functioned well in their society, albeit using different modes of coping.

Therefore, from the medical description of schizophrenia it follows that the psychological states involved in shamanism are not the same as those involved in schizophrenia.[8]

The allegation that the shaman is actually a schizophrenic who has used his or her experience for personal and social benefit has led some researchers to take a

---

* Their responses were compared to those of fifty-two Apaches who were not shamans and seven Apaches who believed themselves to be shamans but who were not so designated in their communities. All three groups were composed of both male and female subjects.
† The pseudo-shamans showed less personality integration than either the shamans or the nonshamans.[9]

romantic notion of schizophrenic disturbances. They claim that the schizophrenic should be looked upon as an "inner voyager" and allowed to proceed with the trip. Instead of hospitalizing and medicating schizophrenics, they should be treated as potential shamans and guided through their hallucinations and delusions until a degree of personal and social integration has been attained. It is true that some case studies have been presented in which this successful guidance appears to have taken place. However, a close examination of these accounts suggests that these individuals actually suffered from a far less serious disorder. Most schizophrenics are, indeed, voyagers, but they give the impression that they are adrift on a ship that does not know where it is going and which never reaches port.

Mediums and Schizophrenia

When we turn to diviners, spiritists, and mediums, we find a somewhat greater concordance with the psychiatric descriptions of schizophrenic delusions than is true of shamans. For example, the schizophrenic claim that one's "feelings, impulses, thoughts, or actions are not one's own but are imposed by some external force" could apply to the medium's possession states. But like the shaman's altered state, the medium's altered state represents a small percentage of his or her daily existence. Mediums and shamans generally occupy themselves with practical tasks of the ordinary world—raising families, preparing food, conducting business enterprises. Schizophrenics are in altered states most of the time and are generally unable to function well in the domain of "ordinary reality." Nor are their altered states culturally approved and appropriate to the social group, as are those of the shamans and mediums engaged in healing functions.

Eileen Garrett was the most celebrated medium of the twentieth century and the one who made herself available for the greatest amount of testing by psychiatrists, psychologists, and parapsychologists. Her main spirit guides were Uvani, who claimed to be a soldier from India; Abduhl Latif, supposedly an Arabian physician; Tehotah, who stated that he was a symbol of creation; and Rama, purportedly a symbol of the life force. Ira Progoff, a psychiatrist, extensively interviewed Garrett and each of her spirit guides. He observed that Tehotah and Rama emerged from a deeper level of consciousness than did the other two spirits, and that they resembled the "archetypes" or universal symbols written about by Carl Jung. Progoff felt that Garrett was a highly complex person who used her mediumship and spirits in an ingenious way to obtain personality integration.[10]

It is the purposeful and goal-directed use of altered states by diviners, spiritists, and mediums that further differentiates them from schizophrenics. Their contact with spirits can lead to personal growth or to assistance for those seeking healing, information, or comfort. The spirits themselves represent extraordinary reality, in a realm either outside the medium's personality or deep within the medium's psyche. Many psychotherapists have observed the emergence of "subpersonalities" in their work with clients during hypnosis, guided imagery, or emotional catharsis. Most of us know individuals whose personality seems to change drastically when they are under the influence of alcohol. There is the shy person who, after a few drinks, flirts with every woman or man who passes by. There are individuals who are usually quiet except at a party, when they begin to talk and laugh endlessly after drinking. These are common examples of a subpersonality taking over once the conditions have been produced which allow this outlet. In cases of multiple personality, subpersonalities assume identities of their own and will often engage in outrageous experiences of which the person has no knowledge. Fortunately, for most of us, our subpersonalities do not assume such autonomous power.

Subpersonalities often emerge in hypnosis. In one study, seventy-eight students were hypnotized, after it had been determined that they could enter altered states of consciousness quite easily and go into deep hypnotic states. They were requested to go back to an age preceding their births and be somebody else. This was an easy task for thirty-two of the students—and psychiatric interviews revealed that they were psychologically healthier than those who were not able to produce secondary personalities.[11] Did the hypnotized students manifest subpersonalities? Past lives? Spirit entities? Any or all of these possibilities might be valid and further investigations are needed to produce more data. In the meantime, it should be apparent that mediums and other individuals who incorporate spirits are not necessarily emotionally disturbed and are in most instances creative, psychologically healthy persons.

It should also be noted that one does not have to enter an altered state of consciousness to diagnose or to cure. Nonshamanic tribal healers, such as herbalists, do not usually enter altered states to heal. Mediums and shamans, however, have obtained their status due, in part, to their belief—and that of those they serve—that information about health is available to them while entranced that is not available to ordinary people.

To obtain this information, mediums incorporate spirits. Shamans have a wider repertoire of options, depending upon their training and cultural background. Larry Peters and Douglas Price-Williams studied forty-two societies from four different cultural areas to determine the range of shamanic states of consciousness and what the states had in common.[12] They identified the common elements in most of these states as voluntary control of the beginning and termination of the state, accurate recall of the experience, and the ability to communicate with spectators during the state. An example of the last factor is the Jivaro shaman of the Amazon Valley. Although under the influence of mind-altering plants, the shaman engages in cupping and sucking activities, appearing to remove the offending object from the client's body and discussing the process. Even among diviners, spiritists, and mediums, interactions and communication with spectators is common. During voodoo possession in Haiti, the spirit will frequently talk, laugh, joke, and flirt with members of the congregation. This interchange indicates that there is a great deal of role playing in these ceremonies. However, shamans were probably the world's first performing artists—and this legacy can still be observed among both shamans and spiritists.

Chapter 15

Toward a Healthy Planet

In 1975, the World Health Organization (WHO) pledged itself to an ambitious goal—the provision of worldwide health care by the year 2000. Since 80 to 85 percent of the world's population relies on other than allopathic systems of healing, WHO realized that this goal was beyond the scope of personnel trained in Western medicine. So WHO embarked on an unorthodox approach that involved the training of native health auxiliaries, midwives, and indigenous healers. Halfdan Mahler, the director-general of WHO, wrote in the November 1977 issue of *World Health* that the utilization of native health care providers "may seem very disagreeable to some policy makers, but if the solution is the right one to help people, we should have the courage to insist that this is the best policy in the long run." In 1972, WHO had already held a conference to stimulate the training and utilization of native birth attendants.

In 1977, WHO adopted a resolution urging governments "to give adequate importance to the utilization of their traditional systems of medicine." The agency has embarked on an investigation of herbal remedies in several countries, an about-face from the laws enacted in British Africa during the mid-1800s that imposed criminal

187

penalties for the preparation of herbal medicines, and the missionaries' injunctions in the 1800s and early 1900s that herbalists were "unscientific" and "unhygienic."

Perhaps as a result of WHO's increasing support for native health practitioners, as well as of the extraordinary cost of health care in the United States, in 1980 the American Medical Association revised its code of ethics and gave physicians permission to consult with, take referrals from, and make referrals to practitioners without orthodox medical training. This move opened the way for physicians to initiate some degree of cooperation with shamans, herbalists, spiritists, homeopaths, and other nonallopathic practitioners. However, it appears that shamans and native healers have been more willing to integrate the discoveries of modern medicine than vice versa.

The Navaho, for example, have divided illnesses into categories that require treatment by different specialists. Tuberculosis and appendicitis are considered best treated by allopathic physicians. "Lightning sickness" and "lizard illness" are best treated by Navaho shamans. Snakebites can be treated by either type of practitioner.

The Hawaiian shamans, or kahunas, have practiced a sophisticated form of healing for centuries. It is their belief that illness results from conflicts in mental and emotional energies. They readily accepted the medical concept of germs and microbes, but they believe that if there were no fear or undue tension in people, there would be no disease regardless of the presence of the germs. The main type of healing done involves the stimulation of "energy flow" in the body to break up the tension-induced illness. Herbalists work with the kahunas to stimulate this "energy flow," as it can supposedly be evoked by medicinal plants, parts of fish and animals, and even colored lights, certain types of clothing, and power objects. Diet is an important part of healing because foods such as raw fruits and vegetables are thought to contain a "life energy" that will assist the patients in regaining their health.

Many Systems, Many Models

The different healing systems covered in this book demonstrate the wide number of alternative models of alleviating illness. Obviously, no one culture has a right to impose its concepts of disease causation or treatment upon another. The only exception would be a situation where a society has made a relevant and scientifically demonstrated discovery that could be helpful in another society. For example, there is now a demonstrated relationship between a metabolic abnormality in infants and a subsequent type of severe mental retardation. It is also known that a specific diet, if initiated early enough in the child's life, will minimize or ameliorate this retardation. Western cultures are justified in sharing these kinds of data with other cultures and encouraging them to take appropriate action.

However, Western cultures do not have the right to impose their standards indiscriminately. The European conquerers of the New World ridiculed and persecuted American Indians displaying divergent sexual behavior. In many American Indian tribes, the *berdache* (a French term for an Indian male transvestite) may have had a shamanic call in a dream or vision. In responding to the dream, the *berdache* would adopt the social role and accouterments of the opposite sex, even to the extent of taking a husband. The *berdache* was often regarded as an exceptionally powerful shaman.[1] Even today, shamans and mediums may wear clothes of the opposite sex or incorporate spirits of the opposite sex during rituals. In such a manner, they are considered to be using the power of the opposite sex to supplement their own power, emerging all the stronger as a result.

Shamans also seek power through locating their personal power animal, totem bird, power object, or even their power spot, which might be a river, hill, or tree. Plants are also said to have power. Sometimes the power is magical, as when it can be used to cast a spell or to undo the effects of a hex. At other times it is sacramental, as when it induces a vision or message from the spirit world. Most often, however, the plant with special powers serves a medicinal purpose. A compilation of botanicals used by American Indians uncovered 1,305 species which have been used by medicine men and women in the preparation of nearly five thousand pharmaceuticals.[2]

For many years, the medicinal efficacy of herbs was underestimated; Western physicians frequently claimed that any benefits associated with their use must be due to the placebo effect, the power of belief in a remedy to stimulate self-healing. Recent investigations have demonstrated that this is not the only explanation. Foxglove, an old English folk remedy for dropsy, has become the source for digitalis, a heart tonic taken today by millions of people. Strips of willow bark and willow roots, often boiled, were used by the Alabama Indians to relieve fever, by the Chickasaws for headaches, and by the Klallams for sore throats. The Greek physician Discurides had recommended willow for gout. In time, these trees were discovered to be the source of salicylic acid, the raw material for aspirin.

Women of the Shoshone and several other Native American tribes chewed stoneseed for birth control purposes; it has now been found to contain estrogenlike substances similar to those used in modern oral contraceptives. Some Indian tribes used the jimson weed to treat various nervous conditions; today, chemicals from this plant are distilled for use in tranquilizers and eye dilation.

In 1952, researchers isolated reserpine, the potent ingredient in rauwolfia root, used for centuries by native people as a tranquilizer. Now psychiatrists are using it for the same purpose. Penicillin originally came from the mold found on hyssop leaves. The cinchona bark of Peru has been used as a source of quinine, a medicine utilized to treat malaria. Impecac, another South American plant, supplies emetine, used to induce vomiting in cases such as stomach poisoning.

There is some evidence that American Indian herbs were more effective, on balance, than the medicines brought to the New World by the European settlers. It is estimated that 60 percent of the medicinal plants used by the Rappahannock tribe had unquestioned medicinal value. The European pharmacopoeia was far less efficient. In 1962, the U.S. National Academy of Science reviewed the effectiveness of all drugs marketed since 1938; out of the 4,300 substances tested, supportive evidence could be found for only 40 percent—and in just half these cases could the therapeutic claims of their manufacturers be justified. This shocking discovery led to the stringent testing procedures now required by the U.S. Food and Drug Administration.

In some cases, the procedures followed by indigenous healers were foolish or even harmful. If they worked, they utilized patient expectancy and the placebo effect. This was especially true in the case of aphrodisiacs or love potions, which in various places supposedly included asparagus, carrots, celery, pepper, and hops. However, the history of Western medicine is also filled with examples of folly. Leeches were once placed on the body to suck out a client's excess blood. A more drastic method was to cut a blood vessel to "bleed" the person of excess body fluids.

Essential Healing Principles

The effort to describe the essential principles of healing did not originate with us. E. F. Torrey has identified four fundamental principles in effective psychotherapy which also seem to apply to successful healing, whether accomplished with allopathic medicine or with the alternative and supplementary healing systems described in this book:

1. A shared world view that makes the diagnosis and naming process possible.
2. Positive personal qualities of the healer that facilitate the client's recovery.
3. Client expectations of recovery that assist the healing process.
4. Specific techniques, materials, and healing procedures that are appropriate to the illness and conducive to recovery.[3]

All four components appear to be universal, although many are colored by the specific culture in which the healing system operates. Take point number 1, for example. A physician can give penicillin to any patient with certain kinds of infection and that patient will probably recover. Penicillin does not depend upon a common language or a shared world view. However, some societies believe in illnesses that are unknown to Western medicine—"lizard illness," *mal aire* (bad humors), *susto* (an affliction produced by breaking a taboo). If a client in Peru insists he is suffering from *susto* and if the local physician insists there is no such malady, the sufferer may simply find a shaman who is able to perform the necessary rituals to remove the affliction.

There is also the possibility that a similar symptom may have different meanings in different societies, and the treatment will differ remarkably. Much to the misfortune of the afflicted victims, the Pima Indian shamans will not treat snakebite symptoms, as they are not considered treatable. The Navahos, however, consider this to be one of the maladies treatable either by native practitioners or by Western medicine. As a result, fatalities due to snakebite are higher among Pimas than among Navahos.

The healing systems we have encountered reveal that illnesses are held to be caused by any one of three factors: biological (or physical) events, psychological (or experiental) events, or spiritual (or metaphysical) events. The third factor, denied or ignored by allopathic medicine, is the foundation of many of the native traditions. Thus, not only must the disease be named, but the diagnosis must reflect the shared world view of healer and client to be effective. If there is the proper match, the very act of naming an illness has a healing effect. The client's anxiety is decreased by the knowledge that a trusted and respected healer understands what is wrong.

The second element of successful healing involves the personal qualities of the healer—those that the healer actually possesses and those attributed to him or her by the patient. These personal qualities differ from culture to culture. An investigator of shamanic healing reported that clients were aware of the shamans' "inner force," an awareness that appeared to be therapeutic.[4] Similar impressions were related to us by patients of the healers we investigated.

The third principle of successful healing, patient expectation, was recognized by Sigmund Freud, who observed that psychoanalysis and native tribal therapies both utilized "expectant faith" to induce positive changes.[5] All the healing systems we studied raised the client's hopes through the management of the healing environment, the healing paraphernalia, and the healer's

193

reputation. Studies of the placebo effect provide further evidence for the power of the client's self-fulfilling prophecies. The healer's effort to heighten the client's positive expectations can be just as genuinely therapeutic as any curative technique. The opposite is also true; "voodoo death" has been known to occur when a victim strongly believes that a sorcerer's hex is powerful enough to have a fatal effect.

The fourth effective healing principle has to do with techniques aimed at alleviating a client's problem. Physical therapies may include medicine (e.g., the allopath's antibiotics, the native American's blackberry root); shock therapy (allopathy's electroconvulsive therapy, the sudden throwing of water in a client's face by a Mexican *curandero*); nutrition (Western medicine's vitamins, the American Indian herbalist's cold licorice diet for footaches); surgery (Western medicine's amputations and transplants, Inca surgeons' "trepanning" of the skull); relaxation (allopathic medicine's increased use of biofeedback and meditation; the Umbanda spiritist healer's body stroking); exercise (holistic medicine's recommendation of yoga or jogging; the Native American practice of dancing following "purification" in the sweat lodge); the use of placebos (the allopath's sugar pills, the shaman's "liver of vulture"); and massage (the sports trainer's therapeutic massage, the Hawaiian healer's "Lomi" massage).

Psychotherapies may include the taking of a case history (the questioning of the family as well as the client by the Western psychotherapist and the Haitian "houngan"); emotional catharsis (the primal therapist's elicitation of screaming, the Native American church's peyote chief's encouraging the client to relive painful experiences); suggestion (the hypnotherapist's posthypnotic suggestions, Apache and Washo shamans' use of direct suggestion after focusing the client's attention);

dream interpretation (Hopi healers and Jungian psycho-therapists both looking for archetypal symbols in dreams); free association (Ute shamans and Western psychoanalysts encouraging clients to say anything that may come to their mind in relation to a problem); conditioning (the behavior therapist's "desensitizing" a client to a fear or concern, the same effect obtained by ritual chanting); art therapy (clients' drawings and tribal sand paintings which may both contain healing symbols); music therapy (clients' insights emerging while listening to taped music or participating in a drum ceremony); movement therapy (physical and emotional involvement of the client in therapeutic dancing and in the Salish tribe's Spirit Dance); and role playing (the Iroquois dream reenactment and the client's playing various roles in gestalt therapy or in a psychodrama).

Social therapies may include group therapy (Alcoholics Anonymous and voodoo rituals); milieu therapy (in the West, a disturbed client's living in a "therapeutic community"; in the Pueblo tribe, a disturbed member's being adopted into a new clan); hospital therapy (in the West, psychotics' being institutionalized; in Brazil, severely troubled clients' moving into a spiritist clinic); family therapy (the entire family being seen together by the social worker or by the *curandera*). Regarding psychotherapy and social therapy, the psychiatrist E. Fuller Torrey observes that there are more similarities than differences between shamans and psychotherapists and that the success rate of both is about the same.[6]

Perhaps the factor most often neglected by allopathic medicine is the role of positive patient expectations. The true case history of a patient suffering from malignant lymphosarcoma, a form of cancer, helps to illustrate this point. Cancerous masses the size of oranges were present in the client's abdomen, chest, groin, and neck. The spleen and liver were greatly enlarged, and he required oxygen by mask. Resistant to all treatment, he was completely bedridden and his life expectancy was thought to be a matter of weeks.

Despite this situation, the client was not without hope, because he had heard of an anticancer drug called Krebiozen and discovered that it was to be tried at the hospital where he was being treated. His request to receive the drug was reluctantly granted.

The client's response was astonishing. After one day of treatment, the tumor masses melted to half their original size. Within ten days, all signs of the disease vanished and he was discharged. After two months, however, conflicting reports about Krebiozen began to appear in the newspapers. The client lost hope and the tumors returned.

His physician, however, told him not to believe what he read, insisting that a new superrefined, double-strength form of Krebiozen was to arrive on the following day. Once the client's optimistic expectations were restored, he was given a placebo treatment of water injections. Recovery was even more dramatic than before. He was discharged and continued to be free of symptoms for over two months.

This second remission continued until shortly after the newspapers published an announcement from the American Medical Association that nationwide tests showed Krebiozen to be worthless. Within a few days, the client was readmitted to the hospital, and he died within forty-eight hours.[7]

In this instance, the ailment was serious. The client's hope evoked self-healing but only maintained it as long as the hope was reinforced by the media and his doctors. The treatment was basically a placebo. The hospital environment and the physician were supportive of the patient, but the outside world—in the form of media reports—destroyed the hope that, for a while, sustained him. Sometimes the client has faith in a healer rather than in a treatment or drug. Sometimes the client's faith is in God. In any event, the client's attitude can play a vital part in the eventual outcome.

Integrating Healing States

When the Jungian psychoanalyst Ira Progoff interviewed the spirit guides of Eileen Garrett, he was struck by their masculine identity. He concluded that Garrett's goal in life—to advance her mediumship—required a strong and active character in a world dominated by men. To resolve this conflict, he felt that she "worked out this necessary arrangement with exceptional ingenuity." Garrett herself wavered between regarding her voices as her own subpersonalities and as guides from the spirit world. From a psychological point of view it makes little difference, because they served the purpose of personality integration. Furthermore, they provided her with information with which she was unfamiliar in her ordinary state of consciousness—information found to be useful by her clients.[8]

Larry Peters and Douglass Price-Williams find the shaman's "astral flight" and the medium's spirit incorporation or possession to be highly psychotherapeutic. For these observers, the common element appeared to be catharsis—the therapeutic release of emotional tension. They have pointed out the similarity of "astral flights" to psychotherapeutic procedures such as guided fantasy, "waking dreams," and evoked visual imagery. Each of these can be accompanied by considerable emotional reactivity. Spirit incorporation, according to Peters and Price-Williams, resembles "deep hypnosis," psychodrama, and certain types of creative states. In each instance, conscious awareness or "lucidity" may be lost and emotional material may emerge from the unconscious.[9]

Anthropologists have estimated that there are at least four thousand societies in the world today; about 90 percent of them have institutionalized at least one set of procedures for systematic cultivation of specific kinds of altered states. One of the key purposes of this cultivation is the entry into a sacred world of the spiritual realities underlying or interpenetrating the ordinary, everyday world.[10] State-dependent learning (see Chapter 2) may be a key factor in understanding why altered states are so often used for healing by native practitioners. Because healing was associated with extraordinary reality, altered states may have been considered to be the best way to access those realms.

Spiritism has been used as a supplementary healing system in New York community mental health centers for several years.[11] In addition, a successful project designed to integrate Western psychotherapy with spiritism has been initiated in several Puerto Rican community mental health centers. The writings of Allan Kardec came to Puerto Rico through Spain, where they had made a positive impact upon a group of freethinkers and intellectuals. Referred to as *espiritismo* in Puerto Rico, it focuses upon the medium as a counselor and healer. *Espiritismo* transformed and legitimized the nineteenth-century Puerto Rican *curanderos* and *curanderas* who had been under heavy attack from medical authorities. It was felt that spirit guides could direct practitioners to the proper medicinal plants and could also offer advice to the afflicted.

In one of the mental health centers, spiritist healers and health professionals met twice a week for three years. The first weekly conference included lectures by health professionals and spiritist healers. The second weekly session consisted of case conferences where both groups gave their input regarding clients coming to the center. The group found that the spiritists were highly motivated and committed to their work and that spiritist therapy was more powerfully charged emotionally. The therapy practiced by spiritist healers consisted of rituals and the use of herbs. The clients were urged to develop themselves spiritually; sessions often focused upon the meaning of life and the individual's connection to the cosmos. The client's extended family was often called in, and advice was freely given. The mental health center's psychotherapists also gave advice, but it focused on more practical aspects of the case.

In one remarkable case, a client was seen by both psychiatric and *espiritismo* practitioners. When brought to the center she was given medication for her depression and visual hallucinations. The spiritist brought in four colleagues who allegedly exorcised eight spirits. She was discharged a week later, talking happily about her plans to finish secretarial school.

In several cases the mental health professionals sought out spiritist counseling themselves. One psychologist consulted with a spiritist during his divorce proceedings and purportedly obtained help from his spirit guides to win his court battles. He married again after working through his relationships with the spiritist's help. He reported that *espiritismo* had been far more effective in his case than the psychotherapy he had previously received.[12]

In the American Southwest, Navaho shamans have been allowed to enter hospitals to work with Native American patients, where they would frequently rely on the use of herbs and healing chants. The Navaho shamans learn ceremonial chants during their long apprenticeship; there are about ten important chants and it takes several years to learn just one of them. Hosteen Klah, the famous Navaho shaman who died in 1937, knew more chants than any other healer of his time. It took him twenty-six years to learn the "Yeibichai," a nine-day chant. A chant consists of hundreds of songs; there are chants that are two nights, five nights, and nine nights in length. During the "chantaway," the chants are preceded by various purification rites and accompanied by construction of a sand painting that typically represents the hero of a myth. Then the patient is placed upon the sand painting and is touched with sand from the painting to corresponding places on his or her body. Upon completion of the ritual, the sand painting is destroyed and the patient is sent back to the community, having been transformed through symbolic identification with helpful spirits.

The chantaway is closely tied to the community; great preparation is necessary and hundreds of onlookers attend. The shaman's costs are adjustable but somewhat expensive, as are those involved in the preparation of the chantaway. The outpouring of material wealth is seen as a powerful indication of the community's concern for the sick person.[13] A National Institute of Mental Health grant was once awarded by the U.S. Government to finance the training of Navaho shamans so that the tradition would not be lost. In San Francisco, Leslie Gray, a Navaho shaman, earned a doctorate in clinical psychology and combines both traditions in her work with clients.

The healing traditions of shamanism and spiritism can teach us that as important as healing the sick is learning to maintain our health—indeed, learning to discover increasingly higher levels of health.[14] Whereas Western medicine generally concerns itself with the person only when he or she shows symptoms of disease, the native healing traditions teach that the health of the individual must be maintained through daily practice of healthful life styles, connection to the Great Spirit and to the Mother Earth, and through service to others and to the planet. Moreover, both shamans and spiritists claim that we can never be fully healed until we become healers of our culture and environment. The shamans go even farther, asserting that today all of us from the West have no choice but to become healers and caretakers of the Earth. We have developed armaments capable of destroying all life on Earth and genetic technologies capable of creating new life forms. We have developed the powers once only attributed to gods to create and destroy life. We must now become "persons of knowledge," acquiring the wisdom to be able to use these tools for the benefit of the earth and of humanity.

There are several ways we can become healers or caretakers of the Earth. We can take the more traditional paths, such as those taken by the healers described in this book. Or we can take the path of "planetary healing," becoming positive and transforming influences in our schools, homes, and workplaces and developing impeccability in our ethics and actions. Thus one can be a healer by being a journalist, a teacher, a homemaker, or a street cleaner. When one develops the world-view of a shaman, one becomes a healer in all of one's activities.

In 1984, Rolling Thunder was invited to lecture at Saybrook Institute, the graduate school where Krippner teaches. In his talk, he made the assertion that "we are not in this life for our own benefit; we are in this life to help each other." For many native practitioners, their healing states enable them to fulfill this ideal and incarnate this vision. Rolling Thunder also commented that healing states are entered as "we drum and we dance."

This striking metaphor can provide guidance for us all as we engage in the dance of life, allowing the rhythm of the cosmos to constantly guide our movements, our thoughts, and our creations.

Notes

Chapter 1

1. W. Roll, "The Changing Perspective on Life After Death," in S. Krippner, ed., *Advances in Parapsychological Research,* vol. 3 (New York: Plenum Press, 1983), pp. 183–193.
2. I. Stevenson, *Twenty Cases Suggestive of Reincarnation,* 2d ed. (Charlottesville, Virginia: University of Virginia Press, 1974).
3. C. G. Jung, "A Review of the Complex Theory," in *Collected Works,* vol. 8 (New York: Pantheon Books, 1960), p. 72. Originally published in 1934.
4. C. G. Jung, *Memories, Dreams, Reflections* (New York: Pantheon Books, 1961), p. 306.
5. M. Manning, *The Link* (London: Gerrards, Cross, 1974).
6. V.L. Raikov, "The Possibility of Creativity in the Active Stage of Hypnosis," *International Journal of Clinical and Experimental Hypnosis,* 1976, 24: 258–268.
7. R. Allison, with T. Schwarz, *Minds in Many Pieces* (New York: Rawson, Wade, 1980).
8. Ibid., p. 183.
9. Ibid., p. 184.

Chapter 2

1. J. G. Fuller, *Arigo: Surgeon of the Rusty Knife* (New York: Crowell, 1974).

2. E. A. Rauscher, "Observations of a Well-known Brazilian Surgeon," *Psi Research*, 1985, 4(1): 57–65.
3. R. P. Kluft, "Hypnotherapeutic Crisis Intervention in Multiple Personality," *American Journal of Clinical Hypnosis*, 1983, 26: 73–83.

Chapter 3

1. L.A. Strudler and L. G. Perlman, eds., *Basic Statistics on the Epilepsies*. (Philadelphia: F. A. Davis, 1975.) Introduction.

Chapter 4

1. P. V. Giesler, "Parapsychological Anthropology: I. Multi-Method Approaches to the Study of Psi in the Field Setting," *Journal of the American Society for Psychical Research*, 1984, 78: 287–328. P. V. Giesler, "Parapsychological Anthropology: II. A Multi-Method Study of Psi and Psi-Related Processes in the Umbanda Ritual Trance Consultation," *Journal of the American Society for Psychical Research*, 1985, 79: 113–166.
2. P. McGregor, *The Moon and Two Mountains* (London: Souvenir Press, 1962).

Chapter 5

1. L. Vilenskaya, "Firewalking," *Psi Research*, 1984, 3(2): 102–118.
2. L. Vilenskaya, "An Eyewitness Report: Firewalking in Portland, Oregon," *Psi Research*, 1983, 2(4): 85–98.
3. Ibid.
4. H. Benson, *Beyond the Relaxation Response* (New York: New York Times Books, 1984).

Chapter 6

1. E. Calderon, R. Cowan, D. Sharon, and F. K. Sharon, *Eduardo el Curandero: The Words of a Peruvian Healer*. (Richmond, California: North Atlantic Books, 1982).
2. A.F. Aveni, "The Nazca Lines: Patterns in the Desert," *Archeology*, 1986, 39:33.

3. D. Sharon. *Wizard of the Four Winds: A Shaman's Story.* (New York: Macmillan, 1978).

Chapter 8

1. C. G. Jung et al., *Man and His Symbols* (Garden City, New York: Doubleday, 1964).
2. J. Hyslop, *The Inka Road System* (Orlando, Florida: Academic Press, 1984).
3. C. Lévi-Strauss, *The Raw and the Cooked: Introduction to a Science of Mythology,* J. Weightman & D. Weightman, translators (New York: Harper & Row, 1969).

Chapter 9

1. S. Valadez, "Guided Tour Spirituality: Cosmic Way or Cosmic Ripoff?" *Shaman's Drum,* Fall 1986: 4–6.

Chapter 12

1. D. Boyd, *Rolling Thunder* (New York: Random House, 1974).
2. R. G. Wasson, *The Wondrous Mushroom: Mycolatry in Meso-america* (New York: McGraw-Hill, 1980).
3. A. Estrada, *Maria Sabina: Her Life and Chants* (Santa Barbara, California: Ross-Erickson, 1981).
4. Mushroom Ceremony of the Mazatec Indians of Mexico. Folkways Records No. FR 8975, 1967.
5. P. Furst, *Hallucinogens and Culture* (San Francisco: Chandler & Sharp, 1976).
6. J. Halifax, ed., *Shamanic Voices: A Survey of Visionary Narratives* (New York: E. P. Dutton, 1979), p. 135.
7. M. Eliade, *Shamanism: Archaic Techniques of Ecstasy* (New York: Pantheon Books, 1964).
8. E. T. Hall, *The Dance of Life: The Other Dimension of Time* (Garden City, New York: Anchor Press, 1984).

Chapter 13

1. M. Winkelman, "A Cross-Cultural Study of Magico-Religious Practitioners," in R.-I. Heinze, ed., *Proceedings of the International Conference on Shamanism* (Berkeley, California: Independent Scholars of Asia, 1984), pp. 27–38.

2. Mushroom Ceremony of the Mazatec Indians of Mexico. Folkways Records No. FR 8975, 1967.
3. M. Siegler, and H. Osmond, *Models of Madness, Models of Medicine* (New York: Macmillan, 1974).
4. D. M. Bahr, J. Gregorio, D. I. Lopez, and A. Alvarez, *Piman Shamanism and Staying Sickness* (Tucson, Arizona: University of Arizona Press, 1974).

Chapter 14

1. A. Neher, "A Physiological Explanation of Unusual Behavior in Ceremonies Involving Drums," *Human Biology,* 1962, 34: 151–160.
2. W. Jilek, "Altered States of Consciousness in North American Indian Ceremonials," *Ethos,* 1982, 10: 326–343.
3. Ibid.
4. S. L. Rogers, *The Shaman: His Symbols and His Healing Power* (Springfield, Illinois: Charles Thomas, 1982).
5. American Psychiatric Association, *Diagnostic and Statistical Manual of Mental Disorders,* 3d ed. (Washington, D.C.: American Psychiatric Association, 1980), p. 182.
6. Ibid.
7. Ibid.
8. R. Noll, "Shamanism and Schizophrenia: A State-specific Approach to the 'Schizophrenic Metaphor' of Shamanic States," *American Ethnologist,* 1982, 10: 443–459.
9. L. B. Boyer, B. Klopfer, F. B. Brawer, and H. Kawai, "Comparisons of the Shamans and Pseudo-Shamans of the Apaches of the Mescalero Indian Reservation: A Rorschach Study," *Journal of Projective Techniques,* 1964, 28: 173–180.
10. I. Progoff, *Image of an Oracle* (New York: Garrett Press, 1964).
11. R. Kampman, "Hypnotically Induced Multiple Personality: An Experimental Study," *International Journal of Clinical and Experimental Hypnosis,* 1976, 24: 215–217.
12. L. G. Peters and D. Price-Williams, "Towards an Experimental Analysis of Shamanism," *American Ethnologist,* 1980, 7: 297–418.

Notes

Chapter 15

1. R. Lowie, *Primitive Religion* (New York: Grosset & Dunlap, 1952).
2. D. E. Moerman, *American Medical Ethnobotany: A Reference Dictionary* (New York: Garland, 1977).
3. E. F. Torrey, *The Mind Game: Witch Doctors and Psychiatrists* (New York: Bantam Books, 1973).
4. R. I. Levy, "Tahitian Folk Psychotherapy," *International Mental Health Research Newsletter,* 1967, 9(4): 1215.
5. S. Freud, *Collected Papers,* vol. I, 2d ed. (London: Hogarth Press, 1940).
6. E. F. Torrey, op. cit.
7. A. K. Shapiro, "Factors Contributing to the Placebo Effect," *American Journal of Psychotherapy,* 1961, 18: 73–88.
8. Progoff, op. cit.
9. Peters and Price-Williams, op. cit.
10. E. Bourguignon, *Possession* (San Francisco: Chandler and Sharpe, 1976).
11. A. Harwood, *Rx: Spiritist as Needed* (New York: John Wiley & Sons, 1977).
12. J. D. Koss, "The Therapist-Spiritist Training Project in Puerto Rico: An Experiment to Relate the Traditional Healing System to the Public Health System," *Social Science and Medicine,* 1979, 14: 255–266.
13. D. Sandner, *Navaho Symbols of Healing* (New York: Harcourt Brace Jovanovich, 1979).
14. R. Walsh and D. H. Shapiro, eds., *Beyond Health and Normality* (New York: Van Nostrand Reinhold, 1983).

The Four Winds Foundation, directed by Dr. Alberto Villoldo, sponsors journeys to research the healers of Brazil and shamanism in Peru, and to explore new dimensions of the spirit. For information about the Foundation's programs and activities, please write:

The Four Winds Foundation
P.O. Box 948
Sausalito, CA 94966
(415) 332-1306